MW01613661

Be Love, Give Love
Abby

Blossoming
out of the
Valley

Finding Peace and Stillness with God

Abby Lewis

iUniverse, Inc.
Bloomington

Blossoming out of the Valley
Finding Peace and Stillness with God

The information, ideas, and suggestions in this book are not intended as a substitute for professional medical advice. Before following any suggestions contained in this book, you should consult your personal physician. Neither the author nor the publisher shall be liable or responsible for any loss or damage allegedly arising as a consequence of your use or application of any information or suggestions in this book.

iUniverse books may be ordered through booksellers or by contacting:

iUniverse
1663 Liberty Drive
Bloomington, IN 47403
www.iuniverse.com
1-800-Authors (1-800-288-4677)

Because of the dynamic nature of the Internet, any web addresses or links contained in this book may have changed since publication and may no longer be valid. The views expressed in this work are solely those of the author and do not necessarily reflect the views of the publisher, and the publisher hereby disclaims any responsibility for them.

ISBN: 978-1-4620-0799-8 (sc)
ISBN: 978-1-4620-0798-1 (dj)
ISBN: 978-1-4620-0801-8 (ebk)

Library of Congress Control Number: 2011904555

Printed in the United States of America

iUniverse rev. date: 4/26/2011

Editor: Amy Wescott, Polish Writing & Editing, LLC
    www.polishwritingservices.com

Photos: Lori Larimore, Branson Photo
    www.bransonphoto.com

To my wonderful husband, Tim, my best friend and the love of my life. Thank you, my love, for never giving up on me and for always supporting me in my journey. I love you always and forever.

I~I

"Be still and know that I am God."
Psalm 46:10

FOREWORD

It is with great honor that I have the opportunity to introduce you to Abby Lewis. Over the past few years, I have had the privilege of watching Abby's life impact our community. God's love and character flow out of her deeply and powerfully. She delights in obedience to the will of God, and she passionately implements His Word in the love and service of others. She is intentional about bringing Christ's message of love and restoration to our world. Abby walks what she talks; she practices what she preaches. She consistently lives out her life's message . . . Be Love and Give Love.

I am overwhelmed by Abby's spiritual maturity and insight, as well as her God-given ability to communicate the true, the good, the right and the pure. Abby's motivation to help others stems from a pure heart that has been miraculously transformed by God. Her peaceful presence and genuine desire to encourage others on their own journeys help build faith, hope, trust and depth in the lives of those around her. She powerfully impacts people who are stuck—those locked up in poverty or devastation, locked up in shame or fear, locked up in negativity or anger. She sees their pain and has compassion as she remembers her own painful past from which she has now found complete freedom. She understands how to speak God's love and healing into these lives, how to give them a glimpse into what it is like to freely live.

Abby's life story is one of triumph…light over darkness, peace over anxiety, joy over fear and stillness over chaos. She is a person of renewal. Her message in *Blossoming out of the Valley* is one that renews hope and renews life. Many people are waiting for this message, and there are some who are desperate to hear it. Do you want peace in your life? Do you want calm over chaos? I challenge you to allow God to renew your life as you read and interact with Abby's message. Learn how to be still and hear from God. Learn how to unlock and unleash the riches of heaven into your life and the lives of those you love.

Yours in Christ,

John Baltes
President of the Silver Dollar City Foundation—Branson, MO

Acknowledgments

Special thanks to:

Tim Lewis, Amy Wescott, Lori & James Larimore, Samantha Freeman, Connie & Phil Ensminger, Mark & Ramona Fitchpatrick and John Baltes for all of your hard work, support, generosity and encouragement with this special project that is so dear to my heart. May God richly bless each of you for your kindness.

And above all else, thanks and praise to the LORD, to Him I give all the honor and glory:

"I waited patiently for the Lord to help me, and he turned to me and heard my cry. He lifted me out of the pit of despair, out of the mud and the mire. He set my feet on solid ground and steadied me as I walked along. He has given me a new song to sing, a hymn of praise to our God. Many will see what he has done and be amazed. They will put their trust in the LORD."

Psalm 40: 1-3 (NLT)

CONTENTS

INTRODUCTION

The Day I Turned to Face God

In 2002, I hit rock bottom. I was only twenty-four years old, but I already suffered from extreme anxiety, control issues, depression and numerous addictions. My marriage was falling apart, as were my relationships with my entire family. My thoughts and words were filled with negativity and lies, and I had accumulated major credit card debt. As my problems piled up, they began to manifest physically through severe neck and back pain, as well as numbness in my left arm and left side of my face. I had no love for myself, no joy, no peace and no happiness. My entire life was in complete and utter chaos.

I remember the day that I thought I was losing my mind. I was convinced I was going to have to check myself into a psychiatric hospital. I needed to get away from the noise in my head; I needed to find peace. Feeling lost and hopeless, and frantic to escape it all, I went outside to sit on my back deck. Though I didn't realize it then, this was the moment of desperation that would lead to my freedom. God was about to uniquely pursue me, and I would be forever changed.

Even though I had grown up in church, I had never felt any deep or meaningful connection with God. I didn't know who He actually was, what He stood for or how He operated. Yet, as I sat on the deck looking up at the sky, I found myself calling out to Him. Desperate for help, I remember asking, "What God? What?" Seemingly out of nowhere, a ladybug flew down and landed on my arm. As I watched it moving around, I wondered why, at the lowest point in my life, this ladybug wanted to hang out with me. *What did it want from me?*

I looked at the little bug more deeply than I had ever studied anything before. Drawn in by the black dots on its back, I wondered why they were there. I noticed the shape of the wings—their brilliant red color—and the tiny antennae. I observed its legs and noticed how they felt as it crawled around on my arm. I was completely enthralled by everything about this tiny little creature.

After what must have been fifteen minutes of watching with awe this little creation, I felt something that I had never before experienced—like something had jolted me. A tingling sensation ran up and down my spine as an unfamiliar peace and calmness came over me. I looked around and wondered aloud, "What was *that?*" I then realized that the anxiety that had long-gripped me had subsided during the entire time I was watching the ladybug.

I had no idea where the feeling of peace was coming from, but it certainly got my attention, and I knew that I wanted more. It was so powerful that it left me desperate to experience—and hold onto—that peace, to allow it to drive out the chaos that defined my life. For that brief time, I forgot about all my problems and concerns, and something began to change in me.

Over the years, God has given me clarity and a deeper understanding of exactly what happened that day on my back deck. It may seem strange that God would use a ladybug to speak to me. But in His wisdom, He used the non-threatening wonder of His creation to pursue me. The moment the ladybug landed on my arm was the moment I turned to face God.

Until that point in my adult life, I wanted nothing to do with Him. If I heard the word Jesus, I turned and walked away. Because of all the hypocritical and judgmental people (who called themselves Christians) I had dealt with in my life, I was completely against church and the name of Jesus. I had never experienced the true light of Christ. I hadn't seen—or at least I refused to recognize—His love fully lived out in anyone's life, so I didn't believe it actually existed. I didn't have an accurate view of God's true character.

God understood that I was against the people who claimed to be His followers, and He knew that I had allowed people to distort my view of who He really is. He knew that if someone approached me talking about Jesus, offered me a Bible or religious tract or invited me to church, I would shut them out. But even all that did not stop Him from uniquely pursuing me.

He knew exactly where my heart was, and He was willing to meet me right there. He drew me to Himself with His creation. Though that ladybug may not have impacted someone else, God knew it would speak to me, right where I was, and it worked. That day was the beginning of my journey toward learning the true character of God and developing a relationship with Him.

Even though I had an amazing encounter that day, my troubles didn't disappear overnight. All the chaos in my spirit, mind and body was still there. But as I turned to face God, He gave me the strength and wisdom I needed to start climbing and moving forward on my journey to wholeness. I never had to receive traditional medical help or prescription drugs, never had to go to rehab or attend professional counseling. But, I did have to learn to trust God to guide me every step of the way.

Eventually, He enabled me to blossom out of my dark valley of chaos. This journey began when God pursued me—He sent a ladybug, and then overwhelmed me with a moment of His peace. As I turned to face Him, God's love and power swept in and began a work in me; my life began to change. My journey of healing, growth and transformation has been amazing, even miraculous. Most importantly, I know that if He was willing to heal me, He is willing to heal you as well.

Whether you are in a pit of despair, like I was, with issues too numerous to count, or you—like many people—have one nagging issue or insecurity that keeps you from freely living, God is ready to help you. Just as He uniquely pursued me, God will uniquely pursue you. Just as He brought me freedom by walking me through a unique healing journey, He can do the same for you.

The inspiration to write this book came from my desire to encourage others to move forward on their own journeys to becoming healthy, whole individuals who are able to *be love* and to *give love* to those they encounter. I hope that these pages will help you recognize that God is mercifully and lovingly pursuing you, and that you will choose to turn to face Him. I hope that sharing the ways God helped me heal from my chaos will inspire you to allow God to help you climb out of your dark valley into a relationship with Him that is full of freedom, peace and love.

This book is not intended to be a step-by-step manual on how to heal. Though I will share the process that God led me through, it will not be identical to the path He has laid out for you. You may already be applying some of the principles in this book to your life. Or, there may be suggestions that you are not yet ready to try. You may even encounter ideas with which you don't agree. That is okay. My desire is that you will pay attention to the things that stand out to you, those that speak directly to your heart. These are your golden nuggets.

God used golden nuggets as markers for each step of my healing journey. As I worked through specific issues in my life, God would send me golden nuggets of practical wisdom to tug at my heart, to confirm the direction I was to move and to show me the changes I needed to make to heal. As I learned to apply these nuggets of truth in my life, I received blessings of clarity, peace and gradual healing. I learned that if I carefully watched and listened, God was always there leading and guiding, bringing me one step closer to freedom.

Learn to recognize and apply the golden nuggets God sends your way as you read this book. Don't try to apply everything all at once. Simply start with what is speaking to your heart; then, as you feel led, move on to the next thing that stands out. Allow these golden nuggets to become the markers for each step of your unique healing journey.

Remember, healing is a process, so be patient. We are all at different places on our journeys, and your path will not look just like mine. I share my healing journey with you in hopes that you will allow God to blossom you out of your dark valley into a life freely lived.

Part 1 - Spirit

"Only in God's peaceful presence would my chaotic spirit find rest, and would I find the clarity and direction I needed to heal."

I

Practicing Stillness with God

God turned my spirit toward Him when He sent a ladybug, one of the wonders of His creation, straight into that moment of my chaos and despair. The jolt of peace that enveloped me that day was so intense, and so unique, that I desperately craved more. Experiencing it forever changed my life, opening my eyes to what I now know was God's unique pursuit of me and His offer of unique healing. If you are like I was, you are desperate for help, for solutions or for peace in your life. Whether you have one primary struggle, or many, your heart's desire is for healing and freedom.

In those first months and years after my encounter with the ladybug, I would spend hours sitting still in nature hoping to recapture that overwhelming sense of peace and calm that had flooded my body, mind and spirit that day. Amazingly, this practice of stillness ushered in that same peace and calm time and time again. Though I didn't yet recognize God in it, I knew that I had stumbled upon something powerful and life-changing.

> Amazingly, this practice of stillness ushered in that same peace and calm time and time again.

At the time, I had no idea that God could use nature to introduce me to His peace, and that it would become the avenue by which I began to seek not just peace, but God Himself. His unique pursuit of me through His creation changed the course of my life. And as I practiced stillness in nature, my life began to transform.

Gradually, I came to recognize that God was the author of this peace that I sought. I also, for the first time, began to experience His unconditional love. Through stillness, I stumbled upon another amazing truth—God intentionally reveals Himself to us in the natural world. The Bible supports this idea: "For since the creation of the world God's invisible qualities—his eternal power and divine nature—have been clearly seen, being understood from what has been made, so that men are without excuse" (Romans 1:20). God created nature, in part, for our enjoyment, and through it we can begin to appreciate His creativity and gain insight into His wonderful character.

In retrospect, I understand that God allowed me to discover the practice of stillness in nature, and to experience His peace and love there, so that I would be ready to receive His healing. In His mysterious and miraculous way, He readied me to trust Him. For the first time, I was actively choosing to turn my thoughts away from my problems, and instead to focus on God. Each time I was able to shift my focus, I was overcome by peace. With each jolt of peace, healing took place within me.

As I learned to accept His unconditional love for me, He gave me the strength and courage to turn from thoughts and behavior patterns

> As I learned to accept His unconditional love for me, He gave me the strength and courage to turn from thoughts and behavior patterns that were destroying me.

that were destroying me. I began to understand that, as His child, God really was *for* me, not against me, and that His plans were "to prosper [me] and not to harm [me], plans to give [me] hope and a future" (Jeremiah 29: 11). He desired me to live a life of freedom and purpose. I learned that if I simply turned to face Him, He would give me all I needed to live out His wonderful plan for my life.

As I learned to focus on God through His creation, He empowered me to start climbing one step at a time out of my dark valley of chaos. He spoke to my heart and said, "Come, seek me and you will find me. I will guide and direct you in the path that you should go, and you will heal naturally." That is exactly what I did. I pressed in to God, did some intense climbing and made some life-changing decisions, but I did not do it alone. All of my strength, wisdom, direction, clarity and peace—everything that allowed me to keep climbing—came from being still with God and listening to His voice. God healed, restored and began to transform me into the person He designed me to be.

Have you ever experienced a moment of complete peace and stillness with God in nature, or elsewhere? Have you recognized God's offer of strength, wisdom, direction, clarity and peace? Do you need to shift your focus? What is keeping you from taking time to be still with God? What changes do you need to be willing to make to begin a practice of stillness?

God desires to heal and restore all of us, no matter where we are on our journeys or how deep we are in our dark valleys. Learning to be still before God is the foundation of our delivery and our freedom. When we truly begin to "be still and know that [*He*] is God" (Psalm 46:10), our lives will begin to transform. We cannot rest in the presence of God and walk away unchanged—He specializes in our complete restoration. And, we can approach God with confidence that He will respond to our seeking. God assures us in Scripture that He "will be found by you" when "you seek [Him] with all your heart" (Jeremiah 29:14, 13). We are encouraged to "come near to God and He will come near to you" (James 4:8). Come rest in His presence, and allow Him to reveal to you His transforming power and love.

∼

When we make the choice to be still before God, recognizing our great need for restoration, we open ourselves to knowing God more deeply. As you get to know Him in stillness, your heart and mind will gradually transform and His love, peace and joy will begin to characterize your life. His voice will guide you, not just in times of stillness, but as you live each day. You will begin to walk in peace as you rely on God's strength, wisdom and direction rather than your own. Learning to rest in and be transformed by Him has a profound healing effect on every part of your being.

> You will begin to walk in peace as you rely on God's strength, wisdom and direction rather than your own.

God is concerned with our complete restoration—spirit, mind and body. Walking in His peace is the pathway to your personal restoration and will bring noticeable change to the way you live. People will begin to see something different in your life—God's light in you—and He will use your life to greatly impact those around you. When God restores your life toward wholeness, His work is not done. He will use your restored life to help bring healing and restoration to others.

The time is now. Turn to Him. Rest in Him. Draw near to Him. Be transformed by Him . . . This is being still with God. It is such a simple practice, but it is often a difficult discipline to develop. Yet God is waiting, arms open wide, for us to turn and face Him so He can begin to bless us, to heal us and to free us. You *can* experience His transforming presence and find healing from your dark valley.

> God is waiting, arms open wide, for us to turn and face Him so He can begin to bless us, to heal us and to free us.

The exciting thing is that it only takes a small change of focus to practice stillness with God. Make a simple choice to take minutes, hours or even days to be still with God, presenting yourself just as you are. God is waiting for all His children to be still so He can speak wisdom and direction to them. He wants to bless you with love, joy, peace, comfort and healing. He wants to heal and restore you.

> God is waiting for all His children to be still so He can speak wisdom and direction to them. He wants to bless you with love, joy, peace, comfort and healing.

Author Max Lucado, in his book *The Applause of Heaven*, describes the blessings of practicing stillness with God like this:

> Think about the people in your world. Can't you tell the ones who have been to his mountain? Oh, their problems aren't any different. And their challenges are just as severe. But there is a stubborn peace that enshrines them. A confidence that life isn't toppled by unmet budgets or rerouted airplanes. A serenity that softens the corners of their lips. A contagious delight sparkling in their eyes. And in their hearts reigns a fortress like confidence that the valley can be endured, even enjoyed, because the mountain is only a decision away. Take a trip with the King to the mountain peak.

It's pristine, uncrowded, and on top of the world. Stubborn joy begins by breathing deep up there before you go crazy down here.[1]

I couldn't have said it better. I was going crazy down here, but God touched me in a moment of stillness and began to change me. He was there all along, but I had to be willing to go to Him to find the peace that I so desperately craved. When I chose to respond to God's pursuit of me, I began to experience His powerful deliverance as He led me step by step out

> God touched me in a moment of stillness and began to change me.

of my dark valley. With each step, I found greater peace and more freedom. However, what sustained this peaceful rest was my commitment to practicing stillness with God. I chose to stay focused on God for strength and direction, even as I got further and further away from the chaos of my dark valley.

I am still choosing to "go to the mountain" to spend time with God every day. Even though I now live in freedom from that dark valley of chaos, I continue to practice stillness with God on a regular basis. I still have burdens I need to lay down. I still need direction and wisdom from God. And, I still need His power to help me "take [my] stand against the devil's schemes" (Ephesians

> Stillness allows me to keep my ears in tune to God's still, small voice so He can guide and direct me in the way I should go.

6:11) that are designed to distract and discourage me from finding lasting freedom. Practicing stillness with God is as valuable to me today as it was in the depths of my chaos.

Stillness connects me to God, keeping me joyful and full of love in the midst of any and all circumstances. Stillness allows me to keep my ears in tune to God's still, small voice so He can guide and direct me in the way I should go. Stillness with God is a time for me to lay my burdens down. It is a time for me to delight in and be in awe of Him as I let all my distracted thoughts drain out of me. It is a time for me to focus back on Him, not on the world or my problems. It is a time for me to get so filled up with His love that it washes over every area of my life, flows out of me and pours into the lives of those around me.

During my time of stillness, I simply listen to Him and experience His presence. I usually say, "God, I am here, and I call out to You. Your Word says that You will answer me and reveal to me great and unsearchable things that I do not know (see Jeremiah 33:3). Lord, I desire to know those things. I want to experience you." Occasionally, when I am experiencing deep pain, or am faced with a heavy burden, I will bring that to Him, and then wait and listen for His guidance and direction.

I try to keep a notebook with me so I can write down how He speaks to my heart. At times He doesn't speak anything specifically, so I just relax and rest in His presence, trusting that He is carrying the burdens I have cast at His feet. Sometimes I praise and thank Him for things in my life, or tell Him how much I love and appreciate all He is doing for and through me. But most of the time, I just sit still and listen.

Being still with God will look different for each person. Call it meditation, quiet time or time with God. The important thing is to take time to be in His presence. For you, stillness with God may be experienced sitting in a warm bath, going camping, sitting in nature or going for a scenic drive in the country. You may find stillness while listening to inspirational music or you may only be able to experience it lying down where there is nothing but the sound of your own breath.

> The important thing is to take time to be in His presence.

There are limitless possibilities. What matters is that you listen to where God is directing you to have that special time with Him. The goal of practicing stillness with God is to allow your mind and heart to experience Him more fully—to completely focus on Him and to listen to His still, small voice. In stillness, you are choosing to resist being distracted by the problems and concerns of this world. You are choosing to trust and focus on an all-knowing and all-powerful God. You are choosing to set your mind on things above as you place your burdens at God's feet, and let them go.

~

Think about the ways, if any, you interact with God. Do you ever sit still and listen? Oftentimes, when we approach God, we rattle off our list of troubles, our praises, our requests, but then we walk away, never stopping to allow Him to respond. Consider a persistent, curious child, talking all the time but never stopping to listen. The child asks for help, but never takes the time to listen to the response to his or her requests.

> Think about the ways, if any, you interact with God. Do you ever sit still and listen?

What if this child only came to his or her parent when something was wrong, or when he or she needed something? How much would their time together be enjoyed if it was spent only out of a sense of duty or obligation? How would the relationship suffer if the child only came to the parent with problems and requests, but never bothered to say thank you, to express love and appreciation, or to listen to the parent's wisdom and guidance?

We are often just like this self-centered child in the way we approach God. Though we think we are focusing on Him, we are actually still focusing on ourselves. We make requests of Him, but become impatient and try to solve things our own way. Or, we are quick to talk to God when we need something, but seem to forget about Him when life is relatively smooth. We view God as a means to getting what we want, but neglect taking the time to know Him. We may even go to God only because we feel obligated, or because we have some kind of duty to check in with Him for fear of getting punished.

When we view our interaction with God like this, we are missing out. Though God certainly desires to hear from us, to help us and to meet our needs, our relationships with Him can be so much richer than this. If we learn to be still in His presence, we can begin to discover the depth of His commitment to us. He wants to have loving fellowship with us so that He can heal and restore us, so that we can freely live the lives He has designed for each of us. He wants knowing Him to transform us so that we will *be love* and *give love* to the world around us.

Unique healing, restoration and freedom in living . . . these are the gifts that God has so graciously given me. As I learned to practice stillness with Him, God changed the course of my life. He healed my broken spirit by revealing

> Unique healing, restoration and freedom in living ... these are the gifts that God has so graciously given me.

His true character to me. Knowing Him enabled me to trust Him to guide me to the next step up the ladder out of my dark valley. He infused me with His strength, wisdom, direction, clarity and peace, which gave me the courage to keep climbing. In stillness, in my surrender to Him, He led me step by step into a life of freedom with Him.

Be still and know that He is God. Take time to delight in who He is—our God who is able. As you learn to listen to His voice in stillness, God will show you His way to your complete healing—spirit, mind and body. And as He uniquely heals you, you will be free to live the life He has planned for you. Turn away from self-reliance, which only keeps you trapped, by choosing to practice stillness with God. Enter into His rest, and allow God to prove His ability to transform your life.

2

Accepting Responsibility

As I chose to turn toward God, He immediately impressed on me the importance of accepting exactly where I was on my journey. Initially, I had to accept that I was in a dark valley— a pit of hell—full of chaos and despair. I had to stop living in my past and start taking responsibility for my own actions. For years I was stuck, blaming everyone else for the mess my life had become, then drinking and doing drugs to numb the pain of my present life. It was a vicious downward spiral that led nowhere but deeper into my dark valley.

We must accept that no matter what has happened to us or what our past decisions have been, we have a choice in how we respond to our circumstances. How we respond profoundly affects our attitude and actions. For one thing, living in the past keeps us from moving forward. We can't change the past, but we can learn from it and move forward to a brighter future. Make the choice to accept where you are today, and then choose to respond in a way that brings you one step closer to healing and wholeness.

> We must accept that no matter what has happened to us or what our past decisions have been, we have a choice in how we respond to our circumstances.

Visualize it like this: You are in a deep, dark valley. In this valley, there is a ladder leading to the top where there is a bright, beautiful, glowing light. The ladder is the straight, narrow road that leads to healing and freedom, and the bright light represents God. You are sitting at the very bottom of the pit, covered with a heavy, sticky tar. The tar represents anything that robs us of peace and freedom.

In my journey the tar was fear, addictions, debt, physical struggles, anxiety, depression and a host of other issues. For you, this tar may represent these or something else. All of that heavy tar was holding me prisoner in the dark valley and was preventing me from being the person God designed me to be. I had a choice to make: sit there in the pit, never escaping the chaos, or start climbing, learning to freely live the life God intended for me. You have the same choice.

What is it that is holding you back from experiencing freedom from the chaos in your life? What is keeping you from moving forward? Do you find yourself living in the past, preoccupied with the things about it that you wish you had done differently? Or, have you accepted that you have a choice to make now, regardless of your past, which will profoundly affect your future?

Acceptance is noticing the tar in your life, and saying, "Ok, this is where I am. I can either sit here, or I can stand up and start climbing out." Acceptance is not denying how difficult it will be to stand up and start climbing after sitting in the heavy tar for so long. Acceptance is admitting that you don't have all the answers, that you are weak and weary. Acceptance is acknowledging the tar in your life and making the choice to rely on God to help you climb out of the dark valley. It won't be easy, but it *will* be worth it. The secret is to keep moving forward.

> Acceptance is acknowledging the tar in your life and making the choice to rely on God to help you climb out of the dark valley.

Each step you take up that ladder takes you closer and closer to wholeness and freedom. But, acceptance is also knowing that you won't climb "perfectly." Occasionally, you may slip and fall a few steps back down the ladder. You might even fall all the way back down to the bottom of the pit. But, I can promise you the ladder will always be there, always. So no matter how many times you fall, I encourage you to stand up and start climbing again.

Sometimes the climb will become so difficult that you may find yourself becoming complacent and wanting to give up. You may decide that you've gone far enough, even though you are still covered in tar. Many times, we are tempted to give up when we are overcome by fear that we will not ultimately succeed. Fear is often the thing that paralyzes us from climbing. However, "God has not given us a spirit of fear and timidity, but of power, love and self-discipline" (2 Timothy 1:7 (NLT)). Don't let anyone, or anything, convince you that you cannot or will not make it. Keep pressing in to God and moving forward.

> Don't let anyone, or anything, convince you that you cannot or will not make it. Keep pressing in to God and moving forward.

As you begin your journey, you need to recognize that our enemy, Satan, will try to pull you back into the dark valley, to prevent you from reaching the next step up the ladder. He seeks to distract you and to make you complacent so that you will not find healing, freedom and the power to live victoriously. He "comes only to steal and kill and destroy," but our most-powerful God has "come that [we] may have life, and have it to the full" (John 10:10). God is offering you a life of peace, joy, strength and love. The choice is yours—you either choose to rely on self, which leaves you unprotected from destruction, or you choose to rely on God, who heals and transforms us with His love.

Make the wise, life-giving choice. God's love is the bright light that offers you a life of peace, joy, strength and love. He will enable you to climb out of your dark valley as you learn to trust Him for the next step of your healing. Choose to accept where you are on your journey, and commit to climbing the straight and narrow ladder toward the beautiful, bright light of God, never looking back.

Apply Helen Keller's famous saying, "Keep your face to the sunshine and you will never see the shadows," as you climb toward freedom. Above all, remember that "if God is for us, who can be against us?" (Romans 8:31). He promises to "never leave you or abandon you" (Hebrews 13:5 (ISV)) and that "with God, all things are possible" (Matthew 19:26). Allow these promises to assure you that you will be divinely supported during the climb out of your dark valley. Learn to surrender to God's love and power, and He will direct you onto His pathway to healing.

3

Surrendering

Surrendering to God may be a foreign, or even uncomfortable, concept for you. What does "surrendering" mean? Do you have to give up the freedom to control your own life? Well, yes and no. Surrendering our lives to God is perhaps one of the greatest paradoxes in our relationship with Him. Only in our willingness to release the tight grip of control we hold on our lives do we find true freedom to live and to heal. It is in seeking God's wisdom and direction, not relying on our own, that we will be released from our dark valleys. It is in surrender that our lives will be truly transformed.

> Only in our willingness to release the tight grip of control we hold on our lives do we find true freedom to live and to heal.

Learning to live the surrendered life is not easy. Though I now know that it is an essential key to my freedom, in the depths of my dark valley, I struggled with an unwillingness to be teachable, a resistance to fully surrender control of my own life. I wanted peace in my life, so I set out on my own to find it. I thought I knew what was best for me, so I was determined to make it happen.

My pride and desire to control my own life prevented me from recognizing my need to fully surrender to God, and I was not open to allowing others to show me His truth and light. I had not yet accepted where I was on my journey, and was in denial about the magnitude of my problems. My behavior patterns were destroying me and the people in my life, but my pride refused to let me see it. I was completely blinded to the fact that I was destroying my career and tearing down my body.

The destruction in my life was obvious to those around me, but I immediately shut down anyone who tried to express concern. I refused to be teachable because I was still resisting God and His use of the people around me to lovingly point out how my choices were destroying my life. I was holding on to my pride, even at the cost of remaining in my dark valley. Even though I was not seeing positive change as a result of my own efforts, it took me hitting rock bottom that day on my back deck to realize I was completely lost, completely desperate. I was out of options.

That feeling of helplessness—of knowing no other options—to free myself from my dark valley was actually a great blessing. Rather early in my journey it became undeniable that my best-intentioned attempts for freedom were not working. I needed a different approach. I soon realized, and accepted, that the only way I was going to move forward was to be willing to surrender to God's mighty power and to allow Him to mold and shape me however He saw fit. Though I knew this was my only way out, it was not easy to let go of my attempts—even my failed ones—to find healing.

> The only way I was going to move forward was to be willing to surrender to God's mighty power and to allow Him to mold and shape me however He saw fit.

It is hard to free ourselves from our pride and ego, to allow ourselves to be stripped of the things that are destroying our lives and the lives of those around us. But here entered that "blessing of helplessness." Underneath my stubborn pride, I knew that if I wanted to heal, I had to stop resisting, to commit to being teachable and to surrender to God's pathway to freedom and healing for my life.

So, perhaps hitting rock bottom like I did isn't the only option. Though I would not trade the "blessing of helplessness" that I experienced on my journey, I do not believe that we all have to get to that level of desperation before turning around and climbing toward freedom. I believe that accepting where you are right now—whether you have one primary need for healing, or many—and being willing to surrender to God will stop the downward spiral of your life in its tracks. Willingly shifting your perspective from yourself to God will have a miraculous impact on your life. This is surrender.

Have you ever truly surrendered to God? Are you willing to continually seek His guidance and wisdom for every area of your life? Are you setting aside your pride and staying out of the driver's seat?

Learning to surrender to God and to be teachable have been key practices in my growth, transformation and healing from my dark valley. It is a daily, and ongoing, choice to focus on God and trust Him with my life. As I spent more time with God, I was able to recognize the areas of my life that were stifling my relationship with Him, destroying my relationships with others and distorting my view of myself. As I confessed this sin against Him and others, God proved Himself faithful to His powerful promise of forgiveness and restoration: "If we confess our sins, He is faithful and just and will forgive us our sins and purify us from all unrighteousness" (1 John 1:9).

> Willingly shifting your perspective from yourself to God will have a miraculous impact on your life. This is surrender.

I have indeed been cleansed, empowered to live like Jesus—the exact representation of God's character—by the power of His Spirit. When I choose to walk in this power instead of on my own strength, my life radiates the fruit of the Spirit which is "love, joy, peace, patience, kindness, goodness, faithfulness, gentleness, and self-control" (Galatians 5:22–23). The display of this fruit in my life is evidence that I have been transformed by Him.

~

Changing our focus from self to God will transform our minds, heal our spirits and change the way we live—it sets us free! Be encouraged: "It is for freedom that Christ has set us free" (Galatians 5:1a). Choose to walk in His freedom, knowing that though you will never be completely free from hardship on this earth, God can use every circumstance in your life to prove that He is faithful to you, that nothing is in vain. Trust Him. Surrender your life to Him. He wants to set you free—to empower you to climb out of your dark valley and to transform your life.

Choose to accept the peace that only He can give you in the midst of your climb toward freedom and healing. But, a word of caution: Don't believe the lie that we can be teachable, live in peace and exhibit the fruit of the Spirit on our own strength. Only in continual surrender to God will we live this way. This is the pathway to lasting healing and freedom from your dark valley.

> Choose to accept the peace that only He can give you in the midst of your climb toward freedom and healing.

Remember, Satan is bent on our destruction and wants to keep us stuck in our dark valleys. He is "the father of lies" (John 8:44) and wants to cast doubt that there is actually a pathway to freedom and healing. He is an opportunist who "prowls around like a roaring lion looking for someone to devour" (1 Peter 5:8) and looks for ways to trap us (2 Timothy 2:26). He desires to keep you from fully surrendering your life to God, to convince you that you can do it on your own. He will try everything in his power to keep you distracted from God.

During my journey out of my dark valley, I certainly fell for some of Satan's traps and proceeded to slip back down the ladder for a time. One "harmless" decision snowballed into a landslide of behavior that I thought I was finished with. *What just happened?* While back in the pit, I felt the weight of the tar threatening to overtake me once again. I knew I had a choice to make—either stand back up, or stay there defeated. But because I had already experienced God's ability to free me, my choice was easy to make. I pressed into God, desperate for answers as to what caused me to fall so far so fast. I didn't want to find myself in this place again.

It was in these moments that God more fully opened my eyes to Satan's evil schemes and motivated me to be on guard against them. God made me realize that I had believed Satan's lie that I could go back to some of my old ways of coping with pain without any consequences. Obviously, I could not. As soon as I took my eyes off of God's pathway for my healing, I fell back into my dark valley. But, I was not there for long. Once I turned back toward God, I felt the weight of the tar disappear. He empowered me once again to stand up and climb back out. Turning back to God caused me to turn my back on Satan, and, therefore, shattered his destructive scheme for my life. When we recognize and "resist the devil," he "will flee from [us]" (James 4:7), allowing us to move forward on God's pathway for our healing.

Thankfully, this experience gave me assurance that God's power to deliver me was far greater than Satan's power to destroy me. God proved that He "who is in [me] is greater than the one (Satan) who is in the world" (1 John 4:4). He reminded me again that true freedom comes when we "look to the LORD and his strength" and "seek his face always" (Psalm 105:4).To do this, we must choose daily to surrender to God and allow Him to reveal His unique pathway to healing for us. The moment we become distracted, we invite chaos back into our spirits.

Many external things serve as distractions, but often *we* are our worst distraction to our healing. Often, our self-directed attempt to find relief from what holds us in our dark valleys is the very thing that keeps us trapped there. We seem to fall into this trap most often when we experience a specific concern that appears to have an obvious, workable solution. In these cases, we typically reason that we can handle it on our own. We take things into our own hands. We race from one potential solution to the next, certain that something will provide the relief we are so desperately seeking.

Have you ever gone on a wild goose chase trying to find physical, mental, emotional or relational healing? Have you gone from one therapist to another or one doctor to the next who each prescribes different solutions for your problem? But, when you follow their advice, you end up with unwanted side-effects or other problems? Or, have you sought to resolve a relational struggle, but it seems to make things worse? Or, have you tried every technique you can find to squelch your anger, tame the need to control, or calm your anxiety, but you still feel like a failure?

As you continue down those paths, you may find you aren't much better than when you started. You might find you are actually worse— hopeless, financially-tapped, stressed out, an emotional mess—all because you are trying without success to find something to solve your problem. If you have found yourself in this place, you are not alone. Even well into my journey, I spent a lot of time chasing after solutions on my own strength until the day God broke into my frenzy and set me back on His path—the only way to complete and lasting healing.

After several years of practicing stillness in nature, which had begun to transform my life in ways I didn't yet understand, I was ready to receive God through prayer and the study of His Word. I spent about two years reading and meditating on the Bible, thrilled that the truths that God had impressed upon me in nature were perfectly reflected in His Word. I came to know Jesus, in awe of the gracious, loving sacrifice He made on the cross on humanity's behalf. And, I began to seek the Holy Spirit to help me live according to God's Word each day. I was diligent and disciplined in my pursuit of God.

It was in this context of living that I woke up one day with the same severe neck and back pain I had experienced in the depths of my dark valley. Thinking I had slept wrong the night before, I didn't worry about it initially. However, the pain worsened. Over the next few days it got so bad that I couldn't work. I started worrying about not being able to see clients, about my business, my health and my finances. In my panic and desperation, I went to see a chiropractor who had helped me in the past. However, with each adjustment the pain got worse.

Finally, I went to another doctor, but still there was no relief. I tried a third doctor who sent me for an MRI, which showed no significant problems. After several weeks and hundreds of dollars in medical bills, I discovered that the only time I had any relief from the pain was when I was lying flat on my back, completely still. One day as I was lying there, I cried out to God asking if my career as a massage therapist was over. In my spirit, I clearly heard Him say, "Be still. Be still."

> In my spirit, I clearly heard Him say, "Be still. Be still."

I realized in that moment that I had been neglecting the very thing that had been the foundation of my healing—practicing stillness in God's presence. Though the spiritual disciplines of prayer and Bible study that I had adopted over the previous couple of years were important, even imperative, for my growth and transformation, I had stopped resting in God. Somewhere, the focus of my relationship with God had become about me doing instead of me receiving and responding to Him. Instead of seeking Him for direction, I had been relying on my own instincts and ability to "solve" my problems. Obviously, this was not working; my spirit was not at rest. And my chaotic spirit led to chaotic attempts to find healing for my pain.

The chaos, I was beginning to understand, was simply the natural by-product of living by my own agenda instead of taking time to first be still in His presence. This was a powerful realization: Only in His peaceful presence would my chaotic spirit find rest, and would I find the clarity and direction I needed to heal. I had to be still.

Thankfully, the pain in my back forced me to rest. It required me to be physically still, but in that, it also opened up space for my spirit to quiet as well. As I spent time in stillness, I recognized how little I had been seeking God's direction in the previous weeks. This shift in focus had caused me to stray from God's pathway to my healing. I wanted to get back on track. In acceptance of my great need of

> As I put all my trust in God's desire and ability to heal me, the peaceful calm in my spirit returned.

His direction, I was able to release my fear and frustration as I surrendered to Him. As I put all my trust in God's desire and ability to heal me, the peaceful calm in my spirit returned.

Once I surrendered to Him, amazing things began to happen. Over the next week God revealed and confirmed a new direction for my physical healing—two different people mentioned a particular doctor's name to me, I received something in the mail from his practice and then I had a dream about seeing him. I felt all of these things were confirmation from God that this doctor, a naturalist, would be the pathway to healing for the pain I had been experiencing in my back and neck. I had great peace about seeing this doctor and vowed to prayerfully follow his advice, knowing that God had opened this door of healing for me.

The day of my visit with the new doctor arrived. The receptionist asked for my contact information, and when I told her my street name— Blossom Valley Road—she replied, "That is beautiful. You should write a book." It was such a strange comment coming from a woman I had never met, much less spoken to, and I was perplexed that she would suggest it. Amazingly, God had already put it on my heart to write a book called *Blossoming out of the Valley*, inspired by my journey out of such a dark valley while living on that street. This was the first thing

God used to confirm that someday I would write this book, and I was also fairly certain that I was at just the right doctor's office.

When I saw the doctor, he first focused on my diet. He helped me to see the ways that it was out of balance, confirming the conviction that God had recently given me about the imbalances in my food intake. For the next thirty minutes the doctor questioned me about various issues in my life, and as I sat crying in the examination room, I realized I still had deep, emotional pain that I had not yet dealt with. To my surprise, the doctor suggested that I write a gratitude letter in order to help heal a specific strained relationship that was contributing to my emotional unrest.

The doctor's instructions that day suggested to me that being a healthy, whole person was much more than being free from physical pain. In order to be truly free, I needed to examine my health in all aspects of my life—spiritual, emotional, relational, mental and physical. When I left the doctor's office, I was confident that deep and lasting healing was coming to my spirit, mind and body.

> In order to be truly free, I needed to examine my health in all aspects of my life—spiritual, emotional, relational, mental and physical.

Nonetheless, I started feeling fearful about my financial situation on the drive home from the doctor's office. Because of my physical pain, I had been unable to work the hours necessary to provide a steady income for our family. In the midst of the fear, however, I made the choice to pray and trust God to be my provider. Later that afternoon, my husband's previous boss showed up at our door. He told my husband that he was in a bind at work and really needed his help for about a month; he would be able to pay him $18 an hour.

> In the midst of the fear, however, I made the choice to pray and trust God to be my provider.

I started praying that my husband would see this as a blessing and accept the job offer. He was already working one full-time job, so I knew it would be a big sacrifice for him to take on overtime hours. When he agreed to take the job, I felt God say, "Now rest and heal; I have taken care of your finances." So, for the next couple of weeks, I did just that. I immediately changed my diet, wrote the gratitude letter and continued to rest and be still with God every chance I got. With just these few changes, God healed me from the terrible back and neck pain. Within just a few short weeks, I gradually began working again, and I haven't had any problems with neck and back pain since.

I am so thankful for this healing experience on my life journey. It unveiled and confirmed what I believe to be the most basic and foundational element of God's transforming work in us . . . to be still in His presence. In order to find true and lasting healing and renewal, we must not only know God by the active practices of reading His Word and praying to Him, but also in the practice of receiving His presence—resting with Him, being still.

It seems that in our hectic, results-oriented "now-culture," the spiritual discipline of practicing stillness with God has gotten lost. And the equally important disciplines of reading the Bible, spending time in prayer, going to church, and even serving others are oftentimes reduced to spiritual tasks to complete. If we desire to experience the fullness of God's transforming power in our lives, we must bring these spiritual disciplines into balance by learning to practice stillness with God. It is from a still, quiet spirit that God is most clearly heard and from where we find the courage to surrender our lives to Him. This is where we find our pathways to healing and are transformed.

Do you think you are on the right path to healing? In your search for answers, have you stopped to ask the all-knowing God what your unique pathway to healing is? Have you stopped to be still and find the peace of God, or are you busy with spiritual tasks?

If you aren't seeing results or you have a chaotic spirit, then you may not be on the path to healing that God has in store for you. I am not suggesting that you will have to stop everything you are doing and go another direction entirely. What I am suggesting, however, is that you take time to be still and wait patiently as you ask God to reveal His pathway for your healing. Stop relying only on yourself to make decisions about your next steps. Learn to surrender, making decisions based on

> Learn to surrender, making decisions based on the peace and direction of God, who desires to guide you onto the correct path for each aspect of your healing.

the peace and direction of God, who desires to guide you onto the correct path for each aspect of your healing.

Let go and learn to trust Him to lead you to the next step in your journey to healing and wholeness. You have this book in front of you; allow God to speak to you through it, and ask Him to reveal the next pathway He would have you take. My pathway brought about profound healing of spirit, mind and body in my life and relationships. Your pathway won't look just like mine, and may be entirely different from what you expect. But, God already knows what will bring you deep spiritual, mental and physical restoration. Trust Him to reveal your pathway to healing and be open to receive it.

God, who offers a life of peace, joy, strength and love, desires to heal your chaotic spirit. Make the decision to spend time with Him so that you will learn to hear His voice. Choose daily to surrender and allow God to do what He does perfectly—love you unconditionally. Be still, and let God's love for you transform your life, bringing you lasting healing and freedom from your dark valley.

> God, who offers a life of peace, joy, strength and love, desires to heal your chaotic spirit.

Part 2 – Mind

"We have a choice about where we focus our thoughts, on what we meditate. Our choice has a profound effect on how we live. Learning to meditate on the truths found in God's belief system, as opposed to the lies and half-truths that often fill our hearts, is foundational to our healing."

4

Taking Thoughts and Words Captive

At the beginning of my journey, God made me aware of the battle that was waging in my heart and mind. I began to see that the nature of my inner thoughts and spoken words were powerful indicators of the condition of my heart. Someone in my life boldly told me I was a very negative person, which hurt me deeply. Though I could not accept it immediately, the reality was that I *was* a very negative person, but was in denial about this issue. The truth was not easy to hear, but it left a lasting imprint on my heart. I started to notice that every word that came out of my mouth was, in fact, negative.

Even though I had had an amazing encounter with God and committed to climbing out of my dark valley, I initially had nothing positive to say about my circumstances, the people in my life or myself. It was as if I could not contain what I really still believed about God, others and myself inside the walls of my heart. The lies and half-truths I was harboring came seeping out of my heart into my thoughts and words. When God revealed this to me, a light bulb came on: If I wanted to stop thinking and speaking negatively, I needed to take some time to tend to the condition of my heart.

> If I wanted to stop thinking and speaking negatively, I needed to take some time to tend to the condition of my heart.

Our hearts reveal our true inner belief systems. Out of our hearts flow our thoughts; from our thoughts we form our words; and, our words spur us to action. The Bible speaks to this truth: "For out of the overflow of his heart his mouth speaks" (Luke 6:45). Much is exposed about who we really are by the way we speak and act. Think about the people you know who are generally joyful, encouraging, loving and peaceful. Contrast those with the people you know who are generally fearful, angry, negative, judgmental or rude. One thing is certain: These two types of people have opposing inner belief systems.

If we want to change the course of our lives—to climb up that ladder toward the bright, beautiful light—we have to make sure that our inner belief systems align with God's belief system. We have to turn away from our old ways of thinking if we want to be changed.

> If we want to change the course of our lives—to climb up that ladder toward the bright, beautiful light—we have to make sure that our inner belief systems align with God's belief system.

The Bible makes clear that our thoughts directly impact the way that we live: "Do not conform any longer to the pattern of this world, but be transformed by the renewing of your mind" (Romans 12:2). Current brain research supports the benefits of this biblical directive to renew our minds. According to Dr. Caroline Leaf, a neuroscientist, this research indicates that a large majority of the physical, emotional and mental health issues we experience today could be a direct result of our thought lives (see Appendix A). Certainly, our thoughts have consequences; they affect the way we live. In order to live a transformed life, we must commit to allowing God to conform our thoughts to His.

Practicing stillness with God and reading the Bible were essential for me as I sought to reframe my perspective, to allow myself to be transformed. As I aligned my belief system to God's, my thoughts and words began to change. Out of the overflow of my changed heart, I began to think and speak positively about my life—my circumstances, my relationships and, most importantly, myself.

This shift in perspective did not immediately resolve all of my issues, but it did bring transformation and healing to my life. It taught me to focus on what I could control—my attitude and response to my life—and to release my tight grip on what I could not. Instead of negativity and despair, my thoughts, words and actions began to reflect encouragement, hope and love.

What do your thoughts and words indicate about the condition of your heart? In general, do you have a positive, hopeful outlook on your life? Or, are your thoughts and words mostly negative? Are you willing to take time to be still with God, allowing Him to reframe your perspective?

Transforming the way we think, speak and act begins with an evaluation of our inner belief systems. Aligning our belief systems to God's cannot be accomplished without the study of His character and values. Reading the Bible and affirming God's promises for our lives are great places to start. An easy way to begin this practice

> Whenever I feel frustrated, anxious, fearful, unlovable or insignificant, I take time to be still with God.

is to purchase a topical book of God's promises. By reflecting on God's promises about His character and commitment to us, we allow our inner belief systems to transform. We begin to replace the lies and deceptions that we hold in our hearts with God's truth, and we are changed.

Whenever I feel frustrated, anxious, fearful, unlovable or insignificant, I take time to be still with God. I read His promises and choose to believe what He says, even when I am tempted to doubt. When I choose to believe the truth about God's character and commitment to us, I am able to walk in peace, trusting that God will do what He says.

For example, I choose to turn from being anxious about my finances to believing God's promise that He will supply all of my needs. Living out my trust in God to actually supply my needs is not saying things like, "I'm not sure I'm going to make it" or "There's no way I'm going to get out of this financial mess." Rather, it is saying, "I may not know how, and it may not look like I expect, but I know that God will supply everything I need."

Trusting God to deliver on His promises does not mean that we sit back and do nothing. Trusting God to deliver on His promises means continually seeking His wisdom and direction, and being willing to do what He asks. We must know and believe the truth about God's character, allowing it to take root in our hearts and to transform the way we think, speak and act.

Allowing our hearts to be transformed is a continual and lifelong process. Even as we begin to conform more and more to God's belief system, we will still struggle from time to time with thoughts and words that are in opposition to His truth. What comes into our minds and out of our mouths will continue to be an accurate measure of the status of our hearts. Learn to be aware of the nature of your thoughts and words, and take action when you realize that what is coming out of your heart is contrary to God's belief system. The Bible calls this "taking every thought captive" (2 Corinthians 10:5 (NASB)). We will either learn to take our thoughts captive, or we will allow our thoughts to take us captive.

Our thoughts and words shape our actions, and our actions shape our lives. They either set us free, or hold us in bondage. We might think of taking our thoughts captive as a grown-up "time-out." When children act out, many parents use a time-out as a means of redirecting a child's behavior. No matter what your age, there is great wisdom in learning to recognize when you need to take time out to refocus.

> Our thoughts and words shape our actions, and our actions shape our lives. They either set us free, or hold us in bondage.

We give our children, and others around us, a great gift when we model the discipline to recognize negativity or un-truth in our thoughts and words, and then to take those thoughts (and words) captive. How would our lives change if we were able to turn frustration, anger or fear into patience, love, trust and self-control? I think we would be amazed at the difference.

~

Sometimes there are long-held beliefs that seem to stubbornly take stake in our hearts despite our knowledge that they do not align with God's belief system, and even our desire to get rid of them. Though not always easy, persevering against these stubborn lies and surrendering them to God will eventually bring freedom from them.

I have used several techniques to help me wiggle free from these long-held wrong beliefs in my life. One of the major strongholds I have dealt with is the issue of fear. As I studied God's character and his commitment to me with regards to fear, I found that the Bible describes Him as my defender and protector, and that it says: "Do not worry about your life" (Matthew 6:25). "Do not fear, for I am with you" (Isaiah 41:10). "Do not be terrified; do not be discouraged, for the LORD your God will be with you wherever you go" (Joshua 1:9). It even says to "cast all your anxiety on Him because He cares for you" (1 Peter 5:7).

God never intended us to live a life of fear and worry; He wants us to feel safe in His care. But knowing this did not always stop me from continuing to walk in fear. I would think and say things that made it obvious that even though I knew what God said about this issue, the truth had not yet taken root in my heart. I would play the "what-

> God never intended us to live a life of fear and worry; He wants us to feel safe in His care.

if" game in my mind: *What if I end up alone? What if I run out of money? What if people reject me? What if I can never get out of this dark valley?* Thinking about and asking these types of questions only stirred up worry, fear and doubt.

But, when I began to verbally affirm what I *knew* to be true about God's character and commitment to me regarding fear, even if I didn't always *feel* it was true, things began to change. Whenever I recognized one of the lingering untruths about fear creeping into my thoughts, I would repeat aloud God's truth: "I am safe in God's care. I am safe in God's care. I am safe in God's care."

I would also visualize something that represented to me being safe in God's care. At this point of my journey, I found great comfort thinking about one of my favorite flowers in God's creation, the daisy. I have always loved the beauty and simplicity of daisies, and have fond memories of picking them for my mom as a little girl. As I pictured myself surrounded by daisies, a symbol of God's care for me, and spoke aloud God's truth, the stubborn lies began to uproot and the seeds of greater trust in God were planted. Healing began to take place within my spirit, mind and body. Within a few days of practicing this exercise, I actually began to feel safe. My heart was being transformed.

We have a choice about where we focus our thoughts, on what we meditate. Our choice has a profound effect on how we live. Learning to meditate on the truths found in God's belief system, as opposed to the lies and half-truths that often fill our hearts, is foundational to our healing.

Many people have expressed to me that they do not know how to meditate, but I do not believe this to be true. Think about this. Do you know how to worry? Worrying is most often a result of negative meditation about our fears or doubts. Positive, healing meditation is focusing on the truth about God's character and commitment to us, and allowing that truth first to transform our hearts, then our thoughts, words and actions.

> Positive, healing meditation is focusing on the truth about God's character and commitment to us, and allowing that truth first to transform our hearts, then our thoughts, words and actions.

I will never perfect this area in my own life, but I continue to move forward on my journey every day. I am committed to taking time to be still with God, soaking up His belief system, so that my inner belief system will be aligned with His. I am also committed to practicing taking my thoughts captive. Only as I continue to do these things will my thoughts, words and actions reflect the love of God to those around me. This is my desire.

Taking time to stop and refocus on God's love and commitment to you will do wonders for your overall health and relationships. Take a walk, focus on something in nature or read the Bible—whatever you need to do to refocus. Stop, breathe and be still in His presence. Ask God to conform your inner belief system to His, to help you let go of the lies and half-truths that you are still holding in your heart.

If you discover you need some help learning to practice stillness, consider using my healing CD called "A Breath ~ in Stillness" (see Appendix B for more information) which is designed to assist you in meditating on the truth of God. Begin today by making a conscious effort to evaluate how your inner belief system affects your thoughts and words. Conform to God's belief system, and watch how love, joy, peace, patience, kindness, goodness, faithfulness, gentleness and self-control will begin to overflow from your heart. You will begin to heal, and your life will begin to transform.

5

Making Balanced Decisions

While climbing out of my dark valley, I encountered countless opportunities to make decisions that would directly affect how well and how long I stayed on God's pathway to my healing. The same is true for you. Each decision that we make is either a step in the right direction, or a step onto a detour.

> Each decision that we make is either a step in the right direction, or a step onto a detour.

In most cases, I have stepped onto these detours when I have made rash decisions that were motivated by strong emotions instead of sound decisions that came from being still in God's presence. Though it seemed like the best, or only, decision to make at the time, I would soon realize that my emotions had deceived me. After learning some hard life lessons on those detours, I realized that God wants me to make decisions that are firmly rooted in His truth, wisdom and direction. And thankfully, He encourages us to seek His wisdom: "If you need wisdom, ask our generous God, and He will give it to you. He will not rebuke you for asking" (James 1:5 (NLT)). However, unless we are taking time to be still in His presence—to listen for His answer—we may have difficulty hearing Him.

In the past, I often made decisions, especially regarding my finances, out of fear. Other times I made rash decisions that were motivated by anger or frustration. Each time that happened, I found myself traveling a road (or detour) full of suffering. I remember crying out to God, asking why I was having such a hard time. My mind was frantic, jumping from one "solution" to the next as I struggled to manipulate the situation.

Finally, I got still, and He spoke to me. In my heart I heard Him ask, "How many more times do we have to go through this before you really understand and learn?" As I sat pondering what I had just heard, it became clear to me: I had developed a pattern of behavior that kept shoving me onto a detour, off of God's pathway to my healing.

I was making decisions on my own wisdom and strength, and was failing miserably. I had neglected to consult God on His truth, wisdom and direction, and now He was gently asking me, "How many more times are you going to make a decision based on your emotions instead of being still for a few moments before moving forward as I lead you?" I felt He was saying, "I do not want you to make any decision without peace in your heart, and the only way you are going to get that is to come to me first. I will be faithful to lead you and guide you in the path that you should go." That was certainly a different approach than I had been taking.

Have you ever made an important decision when you were feeling fearful, frustrated, angry or bitter? Or, have you made decisions when you were feeling overly excited or self-confident? In most cases, what was the result of these rash decisions? Were they a detour off of your pathway to healing?

Do not misunderstand. Strong emotions, whether positive or negative, are a real and continual part of our lives. I am not suggesting that we ignore our emotions; they must be acknowledged. After all, just as our thoughts are, they can be powerful indicators of what we believe in our hearts. Sometimes emotions well-up from the places in our hearts that we have not allowed to be conformed to God's belief system. Other times, they are an expression of heartache, loss or betrayal. And yet other times, they are our response to welcomed new opportunities or new relationships.

> We cannot allow our emotions alone to dictate our decision-making, or we will often be deceived and will find ourselves on a detour.

Whatever the source, however, we cannot allow our emotions alone to dictate our decision-making, or we will often be deceived and will find ourselves on a detour. Learning to bring every part of ourselves, including our emotions, into our practice of stillness with God will help us allow God to direct our decisions.

We will all certainly take a few detours along the way; thankfully, a detour is a temporary alternative path and will connect us back to the main road. The more disciplined we can become about practicing stillness with God, the faster we will make it back to the main road when we do take one of those inevitable detours. Whenever I start to allow my emotions to dictate my decisions, I feel God slowing me down, reminding me to spend time in His presence, before I get too far down the detour. I stop, bring my emotions before God, and seek His direction back to the pathway of my healing.

Take time to analyze what drives your decision-making. Commit to making decisions only after spending time in the peaceful presence of God. Only then will you be able to make decisions according to God's truth, wisdom and direction. Making decisions in this way, instead of out of your strong emotions, will free you to walk confidently down His pathway for your healing.

6

Laying the Burdens Down

As we commit to spending time being still in God's presence, we begin to experience healing from the negative patterns of thought and behavior—the sticky tar in our dark valleys—that have been weighing us down and keeping us from freely living the life God has planned for each of us. God begins to align our hearts to His belief system as we reflect on His character and commitment to us.

As a result, our thoughts, words and actions begin to reflect God's love and peace to ourselves and those around us. We learn to make more balanced decisions that flow from our reliance on God's direction instead of from the powerful wave of our strong emotions. We are climbing step by step up the ladder out of our dark valleys. But, sometimes we still feel burdened. Even in the midst of our progress, life is hard. It is full of new disappointments, temptations to worry and loss, just to name a few. So, how do we deal with these burdens that are an inevitable part of life?

What heavy burdens are you carrying right now? Do you feel overwhelmed, confused or hopeless because of the weight of these burdens? Are you desperate for deliverance from them, for instruction on how to get out from under them?

I have struggled with how to handle various burdens during the course of my journey. After spending time reading the Bible, I knew that Jesus instructs His followers to let Him carry their burdens for them: "Come to me, all you who are weary and burdened, and I will give you rest. Take my yoke upon you and learn from me, for I am gentle and humble in heart, and you will find rest for your souls. For my yoke is easy and my burden is light" (Matthew 11:28–30).

> I would pray and say, "God, I give You this intense burden," but I still felt its weight. I wondered why.

So, I would pray and say, "God, I give You this intense burden," but I still felt its weight. I wondered why. *Did He not take it from me when I asked? Or, did I never truly give it to Him? Was there some part of me that feared releasing my "control" of the burden?* I wasn't sure, but I certainly knew that the burden still had a hold on me.

As I cried out to God for deliverance, He spoke to my heart saying, "Abby, put it on my list." I pondered that for a moment and thought that there may be something to this. When I am burdened by tasks I need to get done, I make a list. The process of writing a list feels so freeing, and something about doing so makes me feel like my tasks are attainable. If you are list-maker, you know what I mean.

I considered what God was telling me and decided to sit down right then and make a list of all the burdens that were weighing me down. I then got on my knees, closed my eyes and lifted the list up, imagining

> I considered what God was telling me and decided to sit down right then and make a list of all the burdens that were weighing me down.

myself handing it to God. When I did that, I saw God saying "thank you" in a very kind and gentle way. He didn't say, "It's about time" or "Why has it taken you so long?" He just spoke gently to me with a sweet smile on His face.

Then I saw God turn around and start speaking to the angels, like He was orchestrating the blessings of peace and provision that were about to take place in my life. I don't know if that is what actually happens, but this was the picture God gave me in that moment to help me release my burdens to Him.

As I continued to visualize this, I found myself being tempted to worry again, to hold onto the burdens. And immediately, I saw myself running up to God and snatching the list right out of His hands, then running to sit in a corner to figure everything out on my own. Finally, I saw the Lord hold His hands up, and with deep heartache in His eyes, He told the angels, "Stop." They immediately stood still, and the blessings had to stop too.

God showed me in this experience that *I* am often the reason that I still feel the weight of my burdens. It has nothing to do with God not hearing me when I cry out to Him, or there being burdens that are too big for Him to carry, or that He is unwilling to carry them. No, it is a direct result of my half-hearted release of my burdens to God, and my unbelief that He will actually carry them.

> God showed me in this experience that *I* am often the reason that I still feel the weight of my burdens.

Even in my desperation to be delivered from a burden, I often still cling to my pride, believing in my heart that I can handle my burdens better than He can. What I have learned is that until I truly release my burdens to Him, I will still carry a heavy yoke and will find no rest. As soon as I start to worry or try to manipulate the situation, I pick up the burden again and snatch the list out of God's hand. As a result, the blessings of peace and provision He has in store for me have to stop. I will know that when I have truly given Him my burdens, I am able to walk in peace and faith without overwhelming doubt or fear. Then, and only then, will these blessings overtake my life.

After this powerful vision and instruction God gave me, I felt that I finally understood what it meant to truly lay my burdens down. After carrying around a particularly intense burden for several weeks, I was finally able to release it to God. In releasing my burden to Him, I received the first amazing blessing, an overwhelming sense of peace that God would work out all the details in His way and in His time. Amazingly, only two hours after giving my burden fully to God, I got a phone call that revealed a major blessing of provision that physically relieved my intense burden.

> In releasing my burden to Him, I received the first amazing blessing, an overwhelming sense of peace that God would work out all the details in His way and in His time.

Though I am not saying that God always resolves our burdens as quickly and neatly as He did this one, I am confident that He can and will handle anything we release to Him. This experience so greatly strengthened my faith in God's ability to carry my burdens, and to provide me with whatever I need, that I created an exercise to encourage others to write their own "Burden Lists," with the hope that they too will experience the easy yoke that God offers us.

Making a Burden List starts with a prayer and includes writing out a list of the burdens you have been carrying. This list could simply be a series of short one-line summaries of your burdens. Do not feel pressure in this exercise to explain in detail your burdens; God already knows every part of them. However, you may find that writing down a longer explanation of your burden—your fears, your pain, your attempts to overcome it—may be helpful in being able to fully release it to God. If this more detailed approach better suits you, I suggest ultimately destroying the description of your burdens as a symbol of releasing them fully to God.

The following is an example of a Burden List that you may use as you seek to lay your burdens down:

My Burden List ~ I give to You, Jesus:

I know that You, Jesus, will help me with my problems and concerns when I give them to You. I have written down all that has been consuming my mind on this list. I give You my list, and I visualize it in Your hands. I know that You are in control of my problems and concerns and are working to bless me, my life and my circumstances according to Your will. I ask for Your wisdom and guidance with the things on this list. I am aware that as soon as I start to worry and fret about every detail, I am not trusting You, and I am taking the list out of Your hands. With the list in my hands, I am trying to figure things out on my own, believing that I can handle it better than You. I don't want to be like that, Jesus. Help me to trust You with my list and not to worry. Each time I begin to worry about the burdens on the list, help me to remember that it is in Your hands. I thank You for all You are doing in my life. I love You.

Examples:
~Reveal to me financial opportunities and how to budget the money you have blessed me with.
~Reveal to me my true pathway to healing.
~Give me greater wisdom and revelation of who you are.

I cast all my burdens onto you. Psalm 55:22.

I trust you with all my heart and I will not lean on my own understanding but in all my ways I will acknowledge you and you shall direct my path. Proverbs 3:5–6

I walk by faith not by sight. 2 Corinthians 5:7

~

My hope is that in practicing making a Burden List you will begin to experience the freedom and rest found by allowing God to carry your burdens. When you release your tight grip on them, you open the door to God's blessings of peace and provision in your life. Learning to let go of our burdens makes us lighter and better able to keep climbing out of our dark valleys into the life that God has planned for us.

> Learning to let go of our burdens makes us lighter and better able to keep climbing out of our dark valleys into the life that God has planned for us.

7

Practicing Gratitude

Life is full of things, both positive and negative, that can distract us from moving forward down God's pathway to our healing. Sometimes these are external factors, like a change in the demands of a job or the possibility of a new opportunity, that temporarily distract us from spending time in stillness with God. But, most of the time, our distraction stems from what we choose to dwell on in our minds.

We too often allow ourselves to focus on the negative aspects of our circumstances or relationships. We may focus on all the things we don't have, or on all the things missing in another person. We dwell on these things to the point that we can no longer see how blessed we really are, or how amazing that other person actually is.

> We too often allow ourselves to focus on the negative aspects of our circumstances or relationships.

I have found myself in this exact frame of mind many times in my life. Early in my journey, even when I began to recognize my negative focus, I felt powerless to change it. However, as I began to understand the harmful impact my negativity was having on my health—spirit, mind and body—I knew I needed a new approach. During my times of stillness, I felt God encouraging me to replace my negativity with "giving thanks to God the Father for everything" (Ephesians 5:20). As I consciously began to respond with gratitude, my views on my circumstances and relationships began to change.

Now, when I become aware of any negative focus beginning to overtake my mind, I re-direct my focus to all the things I am thankful for both in the particular situation I am struggling with and in my life in general. I say things like, "Thank you, God, for the sunshine, for the rain that nourishes the earth, for the beauty all around me in nature, for my family, my husband, my son and my pets. Thank you for my health, my career, for the roof over my head and the food in my cabinets. Thank you, God, for flowers and butterflies, and for the color green."

I continue to thank Him for all the things I have, and for all the things I delight in, until my heart begins to feel grateful and all of the negative starts to melt away. Notice that I did not say that my circumstances or relationships themselves actually change; my perspective changes, though, which allows me to approach my life in a new way. Choosing to change your focus and to practice seeing the good in your relationships and circumstances is powerful.

Once you adopt the practice of gratitude as a way of life, not only will your perspective change, but you will begin to speak and act in a more loving and peaceful way. Your life, and the lives around you, will then be healed and transformed.

> Once you adopt the practice of gratitude as a way of life, not only will your perspective change, but you will begin to speak and act in a more loving and peaceful way.

Do you have a generally positive or generally negative outlook on your life? Do you struggle with negativity regarding certain people or circumstances? Are there relationships in your life that need to be restored?

I have had many amazing moments of healing with gratitude over the last several years. The one I cherish most is my relationship with my father that was completely reconciled after writing him a gratitude letter. My dad wasn't a bad father, but the view I held of him was bad. I only focused on the negative things, so that was all I could see about him until I wrote him a gratitude letter.

I desired to have the relationship with my dad that God intended, the way a father and daughter could. I sat at my computer, prayed that God would allow me to see my dad the way He sees him, and then I began to recall all the things I was grateful for about my father. I wrote the following life-changing letter:

Hi Dad...I know you are at work and probably very busy, but I felt led to tell you some things–things I have wanted to tell you for awhile now. I say these things with a true and sincere heart, so please take five minutes and read this. Thank you for everything you are, and everything you have done for me in my life. Thank you for falling in love with Mom and making me. I am a special design created by my Heavenly Father, and He knew exactly the perfect combination to make me, and that was you and mom. How beautiful it is to think of it that way...I am a beautiful part of you and Mom. I wouldn't be here without you or Mom. Thank you for giving me the name Abby. Did you know that Abby means "source of JOY"? Thank you for your unconditional love and support throughout my life. I know I was stubborn for a while, and very independent; thank you for still loving me and never giving up on me. Thank you for your forgiveness. Thank you for all the financial support you have given me. Thank you for all the extra time you spent in my life fixing things that were broken. Thank you for the work ethic you instilled in me at a very young age. Thank you for encouraging me to always push myself a little more to be better at everything I did. Thank you for your advice. Thank you for your protection. Thank you for always making sure I had everything I needed, and much more, growing up. Thank you for working so hard and being a great provider. Thank you for giving up alcohol early in my childhood so I would not be raised in that environment. Thank you for your discipline and teaching me right from wrong. Thank you for all the sacrifices you made. Thank you for all the love, the hugs and the kisses. Thank you for introducing me to the Lord at such a young age...just want you to know that He is my best friend and I talk to Him, get guidance from Him and read the Bible every day. My relationship with Jesus Christ is the most important thing in my life. Thank you for being you, Dad! I love you more than you will ever know! It is a true blessing to call you my Dad.

The feelings that washed over me at the completion of that letter were clearly from God. The joy I experienced was so incredible that it brought tears to my eyes and a smile to my heart. All the negative thoughts disappeared, and healing and restoration took place in that very moment. The love and appreciation I have for my father now is deeper then I have ever experienced before in my life, and it was all brought about by gratitude.

God does not want there to be division among family, friends or co-workers. He wants us to forgive and to love one another unconditionally, as He loves us. He wants us to be focused on the good in others, to love with His love and to see others, and ourselves, through His eyes. I encourage you to take time right now to ask God to change your negative views about your life and the people who you are in relationship with. If God is leading you to, write that gratitude letter to your mom or dad, your spouse or to whomever you need restoration with.

Don't go another day holding on to those negative thoughts and feelings that are destroying you and others around you. Choosing to turn from your negative perspective will bless you richly and change your life forever. I encourage you to choose daily to walk in gratitude, asking God to give you His vision of love for the people in your life. Right now, take a moment to thank God for all He has blessed you with, and allow Him to heal you through gratitude.

> Choosing to turn from your negative perspective will bless you richly and change your life forever.

8

Removing the Mask

As we continue to allow God to remove the sticky tar from our lives and we begin to heal, we are often tempted to try to hurry the process. We may become impatient with the aspects of our lives that still need to be transformed. We may get tired of the climb and determine that we've gone far enough. After all, we're much healthier than we used to be, right?

We may appear functional enough to those around us that we settle for this height on the ladder. We put on a mask to hide or ignore the areas of our lives that still need to be healed. Covering or ignoring the parts of our hearts and minds that are still unhealthy is a lifelong temptation. We

> We put on a mask to hide or ignore the areas of our lives that still need to be healed.

will always have areas of our lives that we need to allow God to heal. We must acknowledge this fact and commit to honestly admitting to, and dealing with, them as they arise. We have to keep taking off the mask.

Do you realize when you are wearing a mask? Is what people see on the outside different from what is actually on the inside? What parts of your heart and mind are you trying to cover or ignore?

Everyone's mask looks a little different, and is put on at different times and for different reasons. Maybe you are not even aware when you are wearing a mask. I wasn't. Before I started my healing journey, I walked around, unknowingly, with a very pretty mask on. From the outside, I seemed like everything was great, while deep inside I was a complete mess.

I was filled with fear and had a long list of problems that I desperately tried to hide. I didn't want anyone to know that I was weak or imperfect. The pressure was mounting to keep up the image that I was doing fine. Very few people in my life ever saw my weaknesses; I was a master at wearing the mask. Only on occasion did my mask slip, revealing my inner struggles to those around me.

I realize now that much of what impassioned me to keep wearing the mask was not just my concern with what others thought of me, but something much more personal than that. I was filled with self-hatred. The majority of my thoughts and behaviors at the time caused me great pain and suffering, which, if I am honest with myself, I thought that I deserved. I did not believe that I was worthy of being loved.

It was too painful to look underneath my mask, so I kept it secured tightly . . . until, I hit rock bottom that day on my back deck. In that moment of desperation and chaos, I could no longer keep my mask secured tightly. It fell from my face and shattered. I could not hide anymore.

> In that moment of desperation and chaos, I could no longer keep my mask secured tightly. It fell from my face and shattered. I could not hide anymore.

In that moment, I began to experience the overwhelming love and peace of God, which is what ultimately led to my healing from my dark valley. I began to understand that God loved me in the midst of my chaos. He even loved me despite my chaos. I realized that if He could love me like this, there must be something in me to love, something that made it important for me to stop harming myself. I began to see that the way I was living not only caused me great pain, but affected everyone around me as well.

After a few months of practicing stillness with God, I began to experience God's love and healing so powerfully that one day I felt I had to quit using drugs. A short time later, I felt I needed to stop drinking alcohol. As I practiced being still with God, He empowered me and gave me the strength to turn from my addictions. The more I experienced

His love, the more I began to love myself. As that love matured and took over my life, I was able to stop the behaviors that were harming me. I am still amazed that I was able to turn from my addictions and to learn to love myself. But, I know that what may seem impossible to us is possible with God's empowerment.

Take a few moments to think about your life. Maybe you have addictions to tobacco, alcohol or drugs. Maybe you lie or steal, or are addicted to sex, food, prescription drugs or pornography. Maybe you struggle with anger issues that cause you to harm yourself or someone else. Maybe you have a completely negative perspective and a critical spirit. Maybe you hate yourself. Maybe you have insecurities that hold you back. Maybe you doubt your worth. Maybe you . . .

Now, take a few moments to think about the person that you love the most. Maybe it is your child or spouse, a friend or relative. Picture that person in your mind, and allow yourself to feel how much you love him or her, how much he or she means to you. Take a moment to experience the love and joy you feel toward that person. Though we can never love this person perfectly (we are human after all), this is a beautiful picture of the way God perfectly and unconditionally loves us.

Now, think about all of the harmful things you do to yourself, the destructive patterns of behavior in your life. Imagine the people you love the most experiencing all of the pain and suffering that results from these behaviors. Watch them doing all the drugs or alcohol that you take. Picture them smoking cigarettes, over-eating or cutting themselves. Imagine them taking on the anger you feel, or being trapped in a web of negativity about themselves and others. Recognize that their insecurities or lack of self-respect are preventing them from freely living.

This is tough to even visualize. It is extremely painful to imagine the ones we love most inflicting harm or causing suffering for themselves and those around them. It pains God in the same way to see us stuck in patterns of behavior that do nothing but destroy us.

Take time today to sit in God's presence and truly experience Him. Take off your mask and allow Him full access to your heart. You will be so amazed by His power and love for *you*. As you rest in His love, you will begin to turn away from self-hatred and turn toward love for yourself as one of His children. Your life will never be the same. He longs to heal us and to free us from our dark valleys, but we have to take off our masks and make sure we keep them off.

~

After my mask shattered, and I began my healing journey, God brought a couple of good friends into my life who were instrumental to my further healing. Over time, the safety of these friendships allowed me to become completely transparent about my life and struggles. It was so amazing, and freeing, to be able to let these friends see the good, the bad and the ugly parts of my life. The accountability in these friendships helped me keep my mask off, which enabled me to experience healing of deeper and deeper places within my heart.

> These friends saw under my mask, and chose to love, encourage and support me despite what they saw. The same is true with God. To an even greater extent, He sees every part of me, but He still loves me. To an even greater extent, I can trust Him to heal me.

In our conversations, I felt listened to without judgment and encouraged to move forward. Contrary to what I feared, allowing these friends access to my heart and mind was a key step to my healing. Our relationships were also a sweet picture of God's love, care and concern for me. These friends saw under my mask, and chose to love, encourage and support me despite what they saw. The same is true with God. To an even greater extent, He sees every part of me, but He still loves me. To an even greater extent, I can trust Him to heal me.

Do you have a friend who you trust to look under your mask? A friend with whom you can share the good, the bad and the ugly parts of your life? Are you willing to be held accountable to climbing up the ladder out of your dark valley, to keeping your mask off?

We can all benefit from having a friend who we know loves and supports us no matter what. I encourage you to pray and ask God to reveal to you which person in your life you can trust—the person you can be completely transparent with and in whose presence you are willing to take off your mask.

There is no greater earthly encouragement than knowing that you have someone you trust enough to share the dark corners of your life, knowing that they will still love you and help you move forward. This person is a good listener, but is also willing to speak the truth in love; is bold, but gentle; encourages you to move forward in your journey, and is willing to hold you accountable. He or she helps you see the good in your situation, but also challenges you to see the areas in your life you still need God to heal.

> There is no greater earthly encouragement than knowing that you have someone you trust enough to share the dark corners of your life, knowing that they will still love you and help you move forward.

Once God reveals this friend to you, begin sharing your life, trusting that God will speak His truth to you through them. Continue to seek God's presence through your practice of stillness and reading the Bible; this accountability relationship is not a substitute for spending time with God. Nonetheless, share your life with this person with the intention of receiving and applying God's wisdom and direction to your life.

Do not grow weary of the climb, though it will sometimes be difficult. Each step up the ladder, do not be tempted to put your mask back on; be open to God's healing for yet another part of your heart. Honestly address your struggles . . . keep taking off your mask. This is God's pathway to your healing.

Part 3 – Body

"I was unable to properly care for my body because I had not yet accepted my value as a uniquely created being with a special purpose. I had no love for myself. As I practiced stillness with God more and more regularly, my eyes were opened to the changes I needed to make to heal."

9

Taking Care of the Temple

As we continue to practice stillness with God, allowing His great love to transform us, we will experience deep and lasting healing. This healing is multi-faceted and permeates the deepest places of our being. Our spirits heal as we learn to accept where we are on our journeys and to surrender our futures to the all-knowing God, trusting Him to lead us step by step up the ladder out of our dark valleys. Our minds heal as we take time to evaluate our inner belief systems, allowing God to conform our hearts to His belief system.

We learn to make sound decisions, to lay our burdens at God's feet, to practice gratitude despite our circumstances and to keep removing our masks. We learn to love ourselves as we accept our value as uniquely created beings, and as we believe that God has unique plans and purposes for our lives. This love is rooted in God's unconditional love for us and is fundamental to our ongoing healing and renewal. When we accept God's love for us, we open the door to healing of not just our spirits and minds, but of our physical bodies as well.

One thing is certain: You only have one physical body in this lifetime. And, you have a choice about how you treat that body. I am sure you have heard the body called a "temple." The word *temple* can evoke images of a holy place, or at least a place that is to be treated with great respect. Referring to the body as a "temple" demands certain expectations for its treatment. The choices you make either feed your temple life or death, and not only have a physical impact, but can also greatly affect you mentally and emotionally.

As a believer in Christ, my body is the vessel, or the temple, that houses the Holy Spirit (see 1 Corinthians 6:19). It is my job to take care of my body, not just for my own sake, but so that I am able to fully live the purposeful life that God intends me to live. Without a deep sense of unique purpose and an acceptance of God's love for us, we usually neglect the care of our temples. This neglect greatly limits our complete healing and effectiveness. But, when we begin to see ourselves the way God sees us, opening ourselves up to receiving His wisdom and knowledge about taking care of our temples, we are free to live.

> Without a deep sense of unique purpose and an acceptance of God's love for us, we usually neglect the care of our temples.

How do you treat your temple? Do you know which of your behaviors benefit your body? What about habits that may be destroying it? Do you know how to make the changes necessary to take better care of your body?

At one point in my life, I was completely destructive to my temple. I fed it a steady diet of drugs, alcohol and cigarettes. I did not do any sort of exercise, nor did I take helpful supplements or eat a healthy, balanced diet. All I fed my temple was death, and I reaped what I sowed. I had constant pain in my body and felt weak, tired or sick most of the time. The breakdown of my body was also wearing on me mentally and emotionally.

Though I was well-educated about health and wellness, having received a degree in this field, I did not have the motivation to live any differently. I think I knew deep-down that the way I was living was harmful, but I was in denial that my behaviors could eventually destroy me. It was somehow easier not to think about it. At times, I was tempted to believe that I would be less happy than I would be if I had to give up my addictions. But again, deep-down I knew that this was not true.

> I think I knew deep-down that the way I was living was harmful, but I was in denial that my behaviors could eventually destroy me.

As I began my journey to healing, God revealed to me why I was trapped in these destructive behaviors against my temple. Essentially, I was unable to properly care for my body because I had not yet accepted my value as a uniquely created being with a special purpose. I had no love for myself. However, as I practiced stillness with God more and more regularly, my eyes were opened to the changes I needed to make to heal.

Over time, I began to accept God's love for me and soon had an urgent desire to take care of my temple instead of destroy it. I longed to be a healthy, whole individual—to climb further out of my dark valley. But, I was going to have to make some tough choices. Some of these choices were obvious; others were more subtle. In both cases, however, I very quickly recognized my own limitations to making lasting lifestyle change. I could only do so much on my own strength.

> Over time, I began to accept God's love for me and soon had an urgent desire to take care of my temple, instead of destroy it.

I began to understand that God would empower me to make these changes as I surrendered this area of my life to Him. He certainly delivered. As I sought God's wisdom and direction, He led me step by step up the ladder toward the physical healing of my temple.

Learning to take care of our temples is a life-long, and sometimes difficult, process. Long-standing habits are hard to break, but God will empower us to change as we seek His wisdom and direction. Go where He leads you. Start making the changes He places on your heart. Do not wait until your body is in physical crisis to start making changes; sometimes then it is too late. It is much easier to prevent your temple from crumbling than it is to rebuild it after the fact. Accept God's love for you, and believe that He has a unique plan for your life—a life that you can most effectively live in a healthy temple.

IO

Moving

One of the ways we take care of our temples is through "moving" our bodies. The importance of regularly exercising our bodies is widely-known. Many of us even know that for optimal health, we should exercise for at least thirty minutes three times per week or more. But if we know the importance of exercise, then why don't many of us do it?

It seems that there are two extremes when it comes to exercise. First, there are those who narrowly view exercise as a means to achieving an "ideal" physical body. Though there may be some thought to the health benefits involved, the overall motivation is superficial. In many cases, the amount of time and energy put into achieving bodily perfection is taken to an unhealthy extreme.

On the other extreme are those who have no motivation or commitment to care for their physical bodies. Very little time or energy is put toward taking care of their temples. Both of these extremes are out of balance and do not demonstrate a godly respect for ourselves.

Though most of us probably fall somewhere in between these two extremes, I have observed that for many people the word *exercise* often spurs negative feelings. At the beginning of my journey, this was definitely true for me. Exercise seemed like hard work or a chore, so I rarely did it; however, as I sought God's direction on how to better take care of my temple, He gave me a different perspective that eliminated all of the pressure of "exercise." Now, instead of "exercise," I prefer to think of it as "movement." Exercise seemed to imply an unwelcome task, but perhaps movement could be a way of life. I was hopeful.

Somehow, shifting the way I thought about it opened the door to new opportunities to care for my temple. I realized that it didn't really matter how I moved, just that I *did* move. Suddenly, moving my body in a healthy way was not just hitting the gym, but could be anything active that I enjoyed. As I continued to soak up God's love for me during my times of stillness with Him, I developed a greater respect for the body that God created just for me, and I began to *want* to keep my temple healthy and strong through regular movement.

> I didn't want to be unhealthy anymore—to have painful diseases, to age quickly or to be tired all of the time.

I didn't want to be unhealthy anymore—to have painful diseases, to age quickly or to be tired all of the time. I wanted to take responsibility for my own body. Additionally, God revealed to me new ways that I could incorporate movement into my daily living. The freedom I experienced in this was just what I needed to commit to caring for my temple daily. I realized that I didn't have to commit to one specific routine anymore; I was free to move in all sorts of ways. My body would begin to heal.

Do you have a negative view of "exercise," or lack motivation to care for your body? Or, are you obsessed with creating the "ideal" body through exercise? What types of enjoyable movement could you incorporate into your daily routine?

As you think about ways to move your body, think about what you enjoy. Some people enjoy the structure of a regular "exercise" program. Others thrive with more freedom. Seek God for wisdom about how best to incorporate movement into your life each day. Feel free to start out small. You could certainly go for a run, play a sport or attend a fitness class. But, you could also move by cleaning the house, mowing the lawn, taking your pet for a walk or playing in the backyard with your kids. Or, take a walk outside and enjoy God's presence in nature.

Do not focus on how you will keep up this routine for the rest of your life. Simply find something each day that you enjoy that gets your body moving. Not only will your physical health improve, but your mind and spirit will ease as well. Allow God's great love for you to motivate you to care for your temple. Demonstrate the love and respect you have for yourself—a person specially created by God who has a unique purpose to fulfill with this one physical body you have been given.

> Allow God's great love for you to motivate you to care for your temple.

11

Eating Life or Death

Making choices that bring healing to our physical bodies is a vital part of our climb out of our dark valleys. Taking care of our temples gives us the energy and good health necessary to effectively live out our unique God-given purposes. Learning to embrace movement as a way of life is one way that we bring healing to our bodies.

We also must learn to pay very close attention to what we put into our bodies. What you put in your body is either "life" or "death." Obviously, illegal drugs and tobacco harm our bodies and should be avoided – these are "death" to our bodies. Alcohol can also be detrimental so should be consumed only in moderation, or not at all. But, what about the foods and drinks we consume?

> What you put in your body is either "life" or "death."

You have probably heard the phrase, "You are what you eat." But, what does that imply? Most of us would probably agree that this statement is true. But, do we really understand what it means? Perhaps more importantly, does believing that this statement is true affect the food and drink choices we make each day? It really should. After all, how well our bodies function is directly related to what we put in them.

If you are consuming more "death" than "life," then your body likely shows signs of dysfunction. These signs are sometimes life-threatening diseases. But more often, they indicate what we might call "annoying" problems—difficulty sleeping, digestive problems, weakened immune system, fatigue or a host of other issues. We convince ourselves that these types of problems are an inevitable part of life, and we neglect to see the correlation to our diets.

I believe that people are perishing—or at least are not fully living—because of the lack of knowledge about the food that they put into their bodies. It is time to wake up, educate ourselves and take action. You do not have to live a life full of sickness and disease. We are "fearfully and wonderfully made" (Psalm 139:14). God designed our bodies to heal themselves, but often our diets interfere with that process. We must love ourselves enough to change the relationship we have with food; we must learn to eat to live, rather than to live to eat.

> We must love ourselves enough to change the relationship we have with food; we must learn to eat to live, rather than to live to eat.

There is so much information available now encouraging us to adopt a more balanced diet. Take time to learn about the foods that are life-giving. Commit to avoiding, or limiting, the foods or ingredients that feed you "death." As I continued to climb the ladder out of my dark valley, God directed me to information that has greatly impacted the health of my temple. My perspective on food has completely changed, and I now place great importance on feeding my body "life."

Do you make decisions about what you eat based on how those foods will affect your body? Have you ever considered that some of your physical problems may be attributed to your diet? Are you willing to evaluate what you eat and commit to making food choices that give you "life?"

The following is a sampling of the most important information I have applied to my own diet during my healing process. Though I am not an expert in nutrition, I have personally experienced substantial health benefits after making these dietary adjustments. That being said, this information is not intended as medical or professional advice. I encourage you to research the effects of the foods we eat, and to seek God's wisdom and direction on ways that you may improve

> God directed me to information that has greatly impacted the health of my temple.

your overall health through diet modification. Also, it is always best to consult your healthcare provider before beginning any new method of self care.

Alkaline vs. Acidic Diet[1]

Over the years I have studied a lot about the effects of alkaline and acidic foods in our diets. Research indicates that inflammation, disease and viruses cannot live in an alkaline environment. Unfortunately, many of the foods we are accustomed to eating are highly acidic, so many of us may be walking around with the perfect internal environment for disease to flourish.

I have adjusted my diet so that it is slightly alkaline which, in combination with taking care of my spirit and mind, has helped keep my body healthy, free of disease and illness for the past eight years. I consider alkaline foods as "life" and acidic foods as "death." When I keep my diet tipped toward alkalinity, I see my body bear the benefits of health and vitality. However, if I allow my diet to tip more toward acidity, I feel its effects and, long-term, may see the consequences of deterioration, disease, illness and pain.

I have included a food chart (see Appendix C) that will help you be more aware of what you are putting into your body. According to researchers, most healthy adults should aim for a diet that is about 60% alkaline and 40% acidic. If someone is in a diseased state, he or she should start with a diet consisting of 80% alkaline foods and 20% acidic. This forces the body into an alkaline state so it can begin to heal itself. When you look at the food chart, take note of what you eat and where it falls on the alkaline/acidity scale. You may find it helpful to go through and circle the foods you eat on a regular basis in order to determine whether you are getting the right balance of foods, or if your diet is tipped toward either acidic or alkaline. Now, consider how you feel. Do you see a correlation?

If you are having problems with your health, your diet may be highly acidic. Try avoiding highly acidic foods, as they are the ones that can cause the greatest harm. If you do eat foods that are highly acidic, consider limiting them in your diet. Additionally, consider that overcooking your food can

> If you are having problems with your health, your diet may be highly acidic.

cause it to become more acidic and to lose a great deal of its nutritional value.

Our foods are also being destroyed by all of the added preservatives, artificial flavoring, salt, sugar, high fructose corn syrup and unhealthy fats that create high levels of acidity in our food. When purchasing food, it is best to shop along the outer aisles of the grocery store. These aisles generally contain foods that are closest to their natural state, the way God created them. Frozen produce, as opposed to canned, is also a healthful option. Eating more of these foods will bring more life to your body.

Additionally, one of the most important things you can put into your body is water. Make water your drink of choice. Filtered water is typically neutral on the alkaline/acidity scale, so it is a great way to get your body more balanced. The general recommendation is to drink half your body weight in ounces of water each day. If you are not accustomed to drinking water, then start slowly and work up to the recommended amount. To learn more, visit the "Eat to Live" link on my website, www. myjourneytohealing.com.

Antioxidants[2]

Another important component in my balanced diet is the inclusion of foods rich in antioxidants. Most of us have heard of antioxidants, but many do not know what they are and the vital role they play in our health. Antioxidants in foods serve us by removing "free radicals" from our bodies. Free radicals are the natural by-products of many processes within and among cells, including burning energy from everyday living. They are also created by exposure to various environmental factors, tobacco smoke and radiation.

If allowed to go their merry way, these free radicals can cause damage to cell walls, certain cell structures and genetic material within the cells. In the worst case scenario, and over a long time period, such damage can become irreversible and can lead to cancer, heart disease or other serious illness.

A steady stream of antioxidant-rich foods in our diets helps our bodies eliminate these potential disease-promoting agents. Many fruits and vegetables—such as sweet potatoes, carrots, spinach, cantaloupe and mangoes—naturally contain high levels of antioxidants. Make it a priority to incorporate more of these foods into your diet as another component of taking care of your temple.

More than likely, even with good effort, you do not get a sufficient amount of organic fruits, veggies and whole grain foods in your diet. Most Americans don't. I know I don't. I eat well, but I am not certain that I eat a wide-enough variety of antioxidant-rich foods for optimal health. In order to help make up for potential deficiencies, I take Juice Plus+® dietary supplements, which have clinically-proven health benefits. To learn more, visit the "Juice Plus +®" link on my website, www. myjourneytohealing.com.

Key Ingredients – "Life" and "Death"

It is clear that fresh fruits and vegetables and whole grains are packed with life-giving nutrients and antioxidants, but the nutritional value of packaged foods can be a mystery, and sometimes can even be deceiving. Learning to read food labels is another important skill in our quest for eating a more balanced diet.

> Learning to read food labels is another important skill in our quest for eating a more balanced diet.

There are certain ingredients that we should try our best to avoid, and there are others that we should try to incorporate more of into our diets. Dr. Mehmet Oz, appearing on the January 1st, 2006, airing of *The Oprah Winfrey Show,* detailed the Food Hall of *Shame* and the Food Hall of *Fame.* The following is a list of ingredients that, if found in the top five ingredients on a food label, should be avoided—the Food Hall of Shame:

Sugar

When you eat or drink sugar, the sudden energy surge your body experiences is followed by an insulin surge that rapidly drops the blood sugar level—so two hours later, you feel famished and tired. To keep an even keel, replace simple carbohydrates with complex ones so the absorption is more controlled and you experience long-term satiety. "Sugar is supposed to be eaten, of course," says Dr. Oz, "but it should come together with fat or some element like fiber—as you would find in fruit—so you can absorb it a bit more slowly."

High Fructose Corn Syrup

Although they taste sweet, food products that contain high fructose corn syrup should be avoided. The body processes the sugar in high-fructose corn syrup differently than it does old-fashioned cane or beet sugar, which in turn alters your body's natural ability to regulate appetite. He also says "It blocks the ability of the chemical called leptin, which is the way your fat tells your brain it's there."

Enriched Wheat Flour (White Flour)

Contrary to what its name suggests, Dr. Oz says enriched flour is actually poor in nutrition because most of the grain's nutrients are destroyed in the refining process. Instead, he says to look for whole grains and whole grain flours, which are much healthier choices.

Saturated Fat

Found mainly in animal products, saturated fats that are solid at room temperature, like lard, should be avoided in your diet all together. "You can actually use this kind of material for furniture polish—lots of fun things—but don't put it in you," he says.

Hydrogenated oil

To increase their shelf life, certain oils are hydrogenated. This process turns the oil into a solid at room temperature, but also makes the oil unhealthy. "This stuff is great because it doesn't *go* bad, but it's very bad *for* you," says Dr. Oz. Avoid food products that contain hydrogenated oil, often labeled as "trans fats."

Conversely, Dr. Oz lists six foods that he considers to be "superfoods that actually reverse the aging process and keep you healthy." The following foods are a part of Dr. Oz's Food Hall of Fame, and should be incorporated regularly in our diets.

Healthy oils

Dr. Oz says there are many healthy oils, such as olive oil, sesame seed oil, flaxseed oil, grape seed and canola oil. To maximize their health benefits, he says good oils need to be used properly. "Keep it in a dark bottle or in your refrigerator—that's how to keep it healthy so it doesn't go rancid," says Dr. Oz. "Healthy oils are delicate, you have to treat them delicately." He also says overheating good oils during cooking can damage them. "Don't cook the oil, cook the food," says Dr. Oz, "which means put a tiny bit of oil in the pan, put the food in the oil and then put the food with the oil on it in the pan—that way the oil is preserved. It doesn't heat up and it doesn't get damaged by the heat."

Garlic

Dr. Oz says garlic is great for our bodies. "It actually helps the bacteria in your intestines and it also relaxes the arteries and it has a benefit with cancer. It's a great thing to add to your diet. It's present in a lot of cultures – we've forgotten it in America."

Tomato sauce

Dr. Oz recommends eating 10 tablespoons of tomato sauce per week. "Inside the tomato is a chemical called lycopene," says Dr. Oz. "This chemical has a wonderful effect—it's an antioxidant." Dr. Oz says there are added benefits from eating tomato sauce or paste as opposed to plain tomatoes. "A raw tomato is fine, too, but if you get a little fat with it—either with some nuts or a little olive oil and dressing—then it's perfect," says Dr. Oz. "It helps you absorb it better into your intestinal system."

Spinach

Jam-packed with nutrients, Dr. Oz says spinach is out-of-sight. "This is the best thing for your eyes," he says. "It's better than carrots, and a lot of macular degeneration – which is a tragic ailment that affects vision – can actually be avoided by eating these kinds of food that are rich in carotenoids and also have folic acids and a lot of other benefits." Saute spinach with a little garlic and olive oil for a perfect side dish.

Raw nuts

To maximize the benefits of the healthy oils found in nuts such as almonds, hazelnuts or walnuts, Dr. Oz says they should be eaten raw and stored in the refrigerator. "When you roast a nut, the healthy oils that are in there become damaged," Dr. Oz says. "The oils aren't supposed to be heated and damaged—they're supposed to be taken in their natural form."

Pomegranates

Dr. Oz says research on the health benefits of pomegranates has shown promising results. "We've done studies on them showing how they actually can change the way your arteries age—it's a very potent antioxidant. It also probably affects cancer rates, especially prostate cancer, but those studies haven't been finished yet," says Dr. Oz. Not only do pomegranates have extraordinary health benefits – they taste good, too.[3]

Making choices about the types of food we eat is vital to our overall health. It is also important to pay attention to how—and how much—we are eating. It is far better to eat small, frequent meals throughout the day rather than three large meals. Aim for small portions, making healthy choices so that the foods you do consume strengthen you and give life to your body. If

> Making choices about the types of food we eat is vital to our overall health.

you take your time and eat your meals slowly, you will be less likely to overindulge.

It takes your brain about twenty minutes to get the message that your stomach is full. We often eat our meals so quickly that we have already eaten second, or possibly even third, portions before our brain receives the message that we have already had enough to eat. Your stomach is only about the size of your fist. When you overeat, you stretch your stomach, creating potential problems with your weight, digestion and overall wellness. Overeating, or making poor nutritional choices, may also cause you to feel tired, sluggish and unmotivated. But, we do not have to live with these problems. We have a choice to make. It is within our power to avoid these negative effects of an imbalanced diet—the power of our choices.

It is up to you to make the necessary changes in your diet to achieve overall health and wellness. Small changes in diet make big changes in your health. Love yourself and your family enough to start making better food choices. I encourage you to spend time in stillness with God, praying for self-control and discipline. Adopting a more balanced diet is a commitment; it will not always be easy. But, God is faithful and can free you

> Love yourself and your family enough to start making better food choices.

from any of your food addictions or diet imbalances as you surrender this area of your life to Him. Remember, climbing out of your dark valley requires change. And, change is usually not easy. But, feeling alive and healthy instead of sick, tired and in pain will be well worth the adjustments you make. Keep climbing.

12

Breathing Well

Taking care of our temples first requires us to believe that we are worth taking care of—that God desires to uniquely heal us in order to fulfill the unique plan He has for each of us. In order to make the changes necessary to climb out of our dark valleys, we need God-given wisdom and self-discipline to care for our spirits, minds and bodies.

Another less recognized way to increase the health of your temple is by learning to properly breathe. Like so many of our body functions, breathing is something we do automatically, but unless we are having trouble doing so, we rarely consider its effects. Proper breathing can assist us in physically relaxing our bodies, and it can have a tremendous impact on calming our minds.

> Proper breathing can assist us in physically relaxing our bodies, and it can have a tremendous impact on calming our minds.

While in massage school, I realized that I was not breathing properly. I learned that those who suffer from intense anxiety, like I did, tend to breathe shallowly from their chests instead of deeply from their stomachs. Breathing this way overworks the muscles in the chest and upper body area; muscles in this area were not designed to work as hard as this kind of breathing requires.

As a result, the stress put on these muscles and joints typically manifests in physical pain or illness. On the other hand, deep breathing helps prevent this kind of stress on the body and also calms the mind.

Additionally, I learned that when you breathe correctly, the diaphragm actually comes up high enough to massage the lower tip of the heart during your exhale.

I marveled over God's design—with proper life-giving breathing, the hardest working, life-ensuring muscle in our bodies gets a massage with every deep breath we take. How amazing. I knew that I needed to retrain myself to breathe the way God intended for optimal health.

Have you ever evaluated the way that you breathe? Had you ever considered the benefits that life-giving breathing offers to your mind and body?

To determine if you are breathing properly, lie flat on your back and place your hands on your stomach. Breathe normally. Do your hands rise and lower as you breathe? If so, you are breathing properly. If not, you are breathing shallowly, as I was. In shallow breathing, your chest, instead of your stomach, will rise and lower as you breathe. If you are breathing this way, you are never getting a full, life-giving breath.

Do not deny yourself the benefits of proper breathing any longer. Do not deny your muscles the ability to more fully relax or your mind the ability to release anxiety. Begin practicing life-giving breathing today. This begins with an awareness of your breath throughout your day.

When I became aware of my tendency toward shallow breathing, I began to spend time consciously practicing proper breathing. Then, throughout the day, I would try to be aware of my breathing and would make adjustments as needed. As I increased my awareness of my breath, I gradually retrained myself to breathe properly. The more I worked at it, the easier and more natural it became. Now, I have a habit of proper breathing and have reaped many health benefits from it, particularly a tremendous decrease in my general anxiety level.

I also learned to practice deep breathing exercises, which help me relax and clear my mind during my times of stillness with God. I lie down on my back with my hands on my stomach and breathe in slowly, allowing my hands to rise, my lungs to expand and my diaphragm to lower. When my lungs fill completely, I hold my breath for about three seconds before slowly breathing out as I allow my hands to lower and my diaphragm to rise. Once I have fully exhaled, I pause for another three seconds before starting over.

During this exercise, I visualize my diaphragm giving my heart a massage with each breath, a picture that reminds me of God's wonderful design and care for our bodies. I repeat this for several minutes until my mind is clear and my body is completely relaxed. Being in this relaxed state allows me to be still before God, and opens me up to His healing for my life. This is also a great exercise to do when you feel overwhelmed, stressed, or tense and you need a moment to calm down. You may also enjoy doing this just before you go to bed for a more restful night of sleep.

> Being in this relaxed state allows me to be still before God, and opens me up to His healing for my life.

Remember that God created our bodies to function properly, but we can easily disrupt that function when we mistreat our temples. We are wise to not only commit to regularly moving our bodies and to eating foods that give life, but also to appreciate the importance of each breath we take. Learning to practice life-giving breathing is another step up the ladder to achieving more complete health of mind and body. Take time today to breathe well, and find healing.

13

Exploring Other Forms of Healing

Our bodies are all complex, and each unique. Respecting yourself enough to make lasting positive lifestyle change by increasing your movement, eating a life-giving diet and practicing proper breathing are fundamental to the care of your temple. These lifestyle changes are vital for improving your physical health.

There are, however, a variety of other healing services that may be of help in restoring optimal function to your temple. At different times in my journey, God led me to receive other types of care that brought about further, and more complete, healing to my temple.

While in massage therapy school, I was so impacted by the healing benefits of massage (see the "Nurturing Massage" link on my website, www.myjourneytohealing.com), that I knew I needed to incorporate regular massage therapy into the care of my temple. I have not only personally experienced healing through massage, but as a massage therapist, I have seen amazing transformation of body, mind and spirit in many of my clients.

As a massage therapist, my goal is not just to massage away the physical pain; I am interested in seeing my clients become healthy and whole in spirit, mind and body. I desire to help clients find a place of deep relaxation that many people will never experience. Nurturing touch, when

> I desire to help clients find a place of deep relaxation that many people will never experience.

administered with love and a healing intent, can be very powerful. Not all massage therapists, however, use the same approach. If you are feeling led to incorporate massage in your healing journey, do some research on the therapists in your area and ask what type of massages they give. If God is leading you to receive massage therapy, He will lead you to the right therapist for your specific needs.

God also led me to receive chiropractic care in order to realign my spinal cord and relieve the nerve impingement that was causing the numbness in my face and arm. Because of the many health benefits I experienced, I have continued to incorporate regular chiropractic care into the care of my temple. Like massage therapists, not all chiropractors have the same approach. Some chiropractors are primarily concerned with eliminating pain, as opposed to incorporating regular chiropractic care as a part of the client's overall wellness plan. Again, spend time seeking God on whether these types of care are on His pathway to healing for you.

Another thing that God led me to do is colonics, which is a gentle washing of the colon. Considering all the drugs, alcohol and cigarettes I had been putting into my body, you can imagine how toxic my body must have been. In addition, the negativity and anxiety that characterized my attitude, as well as the "dead" food I was accustomed to consuming, were also very toxic. My body was toxic from the inside out. Colonics, which I continue to receive, helps keep my temple clean from the inside out.

Though each of these therapies has been helpful to improving the health of my temple, they were not enough, even combined, to restore complete balance. It was the combination of these—along with better overall care of my spirit, mind and body—that helped me heal and bring balance to all areas of my life. God knew exactly what I needed; I just had to learn to trust Him to show me my pathway to healing.

God will not call you to take the exact same path to healing that He led me to take. There may be things I was prompted to do that are unnecessary for you, just as He may lead you to do things that were never a part of my journey. The most important thing

> The most important thing needed to get you on your pathway to healing is to be still with God and listen to His voice.

needed to get you on your pathway to healing is to be still with God and listen to His voice.

Sit in His presence, and allow Him to show you the next step in your journey. Remember, you do not have to do everything at once; just take the nuggets that stand out to you, those that speak to your heart, and trust God as He leads you along the path He has designed for your unique healing. He will guide you. Surrendering to God and allowing Him to empower you to climb step by step up the ladder out of your dark valley will result in profound healing of spirit, mind and body—healing that leaves you free to live.

PART 4 – FREE TO LIVE

"We are living in the moment—thankful for the past's lessons, content in the present and hopeful for the future."

14

Living in the Moment

As we climb out of our dark valleys by allowing God to heal our spirits, minds and bodies, we are free to live the lives that He has planned for each of us. As we grow in our ability to trust God and accept His great love for us, we are able to more fully appreciate the places we are right now on our journeys; we see that we have progressed, and we are grateful for it.

We begin to view the things of our pasts—even the things we wish were not there—as necessary ingredients for the people God is transforming us to be. We can now look to our futures confidently, knowing that as we rest in God's presence, He is always there to guide us. We are living in the moment—thankful for the past's lessons, content in the present, and hopeful for the future.

> We can now look to our futures confidently, knowing that as we rest in God's presence, He is always there to guide us.

If we do not choose to live in the moment, we will miss out on many of life's greatest blessings. Holding onto our pasts, or always worrying about the future, are strong indicators that we are not living in the moment. Oftentimes, this is a symptom of a deeper issue—relying only on ourselves instead of relying fully on God.

When we depend only on our own strength to somehow redeem our pasts or to determine the course for our futures, we will miss out on what God is offering us in our present. Among other things, God offers to prove Himself faithful, to demonstrate His great love for us and to give us an opportunity to extend His love to others—all things that we, and those around us, will miss if we refuse to trust Him.

For many years, I neglected living in the moment and missed many of God's blessings. This self-focus caused me to miss valuable opportunities to encourage friends or family members when they were down, or to celebrate with them when they had exciting news. By living this way, I was unable to be an extension of God's love and support to those around me. Not only this, but I also shut out many of God's blessings in my own life.

> For many years, I neglected living in the moment and missed many of God's blessings.

In my distraction, I could not focus on God's unconditional love for me, or on the fact that He desired to bring peace and healing to my life. My distraction, which was at its root an unwavering self-focus, kept me trapped in my dark valley. However, as I spent time resting in God's presence, He began to make me aware of my distracted living. Even more, I realized that continuing to live this way would block me from freely living the life God intended for me. I knew I needed to change; I had to learn to live in the moment.

> My distraction, which was at its root an unwavering self-focus, kept me trapped in my dark valley.

Do you practice living in the moment? Or, are you distracted? Are you trapped by areas of shame in your past or are you worried about the "what ifs" in your future?

Regardless of how you live now, you can learn to live in the moment. As we make the daily choice to be still in God's presence, we grow in our ability to trust Him to redeem our pasts and to shape our futures. As a result, we become more content in the present. It is from this place that we can practice God-directed living in the moment. And doing this requires sensitivity to God's leading in your life.

God-directed living in the moment does not always prescribe a focus on others at the expense of self, nor does it always prescribe a focus on self at the expense of others. But, it does prescribe a focus on God as we seek direction from Him on how to live each moment. God promises to guide and direct us when we rely on Him: "Trust in the

Lord with all your heart and lean not on your own understanding; in all your ways acknowledge him, and He will make your path straight" (Proverbs 3:5-6). We will only be content in the present when we choose to trust Him with the unfolding of our lives. Choosing to trust God with your future helps you to rest in the moment.

> We will only be content in the present when we choose to trust Him with the unfolding of our lives.

Take time today to evaluate where you are focused. Though there are many ways to assess where your focus is, God revealed my distracted self-focus by opening my eyes to how detached I was during conversations. I realized that I was rarely fully mentally present when I was with another person. I would look at them with a blank stare—my thoughts were elsewhere. My mind constantly drifted, thinking and worrying about the "what ifs" in my future.

Once I realized this, I made a conscious effort to make eye contact, to stop whatever else I was doing and to focus fully on the conversation. This was not instantly easy, but as I began to focus on God to direct me moment by moment, I learned to fully engage with others. Though I have moments of distraction, I am now committed to living in the moment. This not only blesses my life—I am able to receive love, support and encouragement from others—but also allows me to bless others by extending God's love and peace to them.

Notice how you respond, both physically and mentally, to the people in your life and to the tasks required of you. Notice whether you are distracted or are fully engaged. Your response is a great indicator of your focus. If you are living a distracted, self-focused life, make a commitment today to re-focus on God.

Don't miss out on any more of God's purpose for your life. Your past has shaped who you are today; what happens today is shaping you for tomorrow. Wishing away or worrying about life—not living in the moment—will paralyze you from purposeful living. Take time each day to be still in His presence. As you trust Him to guide and direct you, He will enable you to fully live in the present, freeing you to climb into the future He has planned for you.

15

Setting Boundaries

Freely living the lives that God has planned for us requires being willing to surrender our desires and plans when they do not match up with God's intentions for us. Anything that gets in the way of our climb toward God's purpose for our lives—anything that causes us to head down a detour, that distracts us or that is self-directed instead of God-directed—should be ruthlessly avoided.

Sometimes these areas of our lives are easy to spot. But, sometimes they are masked as good, even necessary, tasks or relationships. Underneath, however, they are poised to keep us in our dark valleys. By taking the time to be still in God's presence, we learn to discern which things draw us closer to His light and which keep us stuck in the darkness. From this knowledge, we learn to pursue the things that God desires for us and to turn from those He doesn't. This is setting God-directed boundaries.

> By taking the time to be still in God's presence, we learn to discern which things draw us closer to His light and which keep us stuck in the darkness.

Early in my journey, setting these boundaries required me to filter my life. God made clear to me the truth of the saying, "You are who you hang around." In my case, the people and places I associated with were keeping me trapped in my dark valley. In order to move forward in my journey, I had to make a difficult decision; I had to filter out the negative influences in my life by completely separating myself from certain people and places. I knew I had to stop going to bars and spending time with people who were into the party scene if I was ever going to escape the control that cigarettes, alcohol and drugs had over me.

When under the influence, my behavior was out-of-control; there was no limit to what I would do. I did things that were not only hurtful to me, but that destroyed relationships with the people I loved, especially my husband. When I was drunk or high or in loud places, I didn't have to face the grave reality of my choices. I could more easily ignore the noise in my head and my heart. I didn't have to acknowledge or experience the depths of my pain. Though living this way numbed me in the short-term, I knew in my heart that it could not heal me. In fact, allowing myself to remain in that environment kept me from taking the next step in my journey to healing and wholeness.

Think about the friends you associate with, the places you hang out, and the things you do for entertainment. Do they bring joy and peace to your life, and encourage you to freely live as God intends for you? Or, do they bring darkness and destruction? Are they holding you back and distracting you from being all God designed you to be? Where might you need to take a stand and filter your life?

During my times of stillness with God, I began to clearly understand just how much my lifestyle was keeping me from living out God's purposes for my life. The temptation I faced by continuing to spend time with these friends in these places was holding me in bondage to the darkness. I committed to make a change, and God began to give me the strength and courage to filter my life.

> I committed to make a change, and God began to give me the strength and courage to filter my life.

I began to limit my association with those negative environments until one day I stopped going to parties and bars altogether. I no longer needed it anymore; the boundary was set.

Though I knew this was the way God was directing me, choosing to set this boundary caused great strain on many of my relationships. Before my encounter with God, my friends only knew me as a fun, crazy party girl. So naturally, when I started ignoring their calls and distancing myself from them, they often got angry. They didn't understand the changes that were taking place in my heart and mind; even *I* didn't fully understand what was going on inside of me.

But, I knew that I had to take a difficult, even drastic, stand if I wanted to be free. I knew that the sacrifice would be worth the peace that accompanies freedom from our areas of darkness, so I stayed true to these God-directed boundaries. Filtering the negative influences from my life forced me to stop hiding behind drugs and alcohol and to confront the issues that kept me from blossoming out of my dark valley. It also challenged me to surround myself with people who positively influenced my life—people who loved me, encouraged me and spoke God's truth to me. Truly, we become like those we hang around.

As I replaced the negative influences with the positive, my life began to transform. And over time, by God's grace and mercy, my friends saw the changed person I was becoming and began to understand why I had set the boundaries that I did. What they may have perceived initially as my rejection of them, they now understood to be necessary to my healing.

Setting these boundaries opened up space in my life to contemplate the consequences of my behavior while in my dark valley. I realized I had been caught in a vicious cycle of "hurt and get-hurt." The way I lived brought continuous destruction to my life and to the lives around me, but I had been blind to the damage. I felt entitled to my own unhealthy self-protection and continued to justify my destructive behavior. I was not free.

When I distanced myself from this vicious cycle, my eyes opened to the truth of the old adage—hurt people hurt people; free people free people. How true. I didn't want to be a hurt person hurting people anymore; I wanted to be free! I cried out to God for help, and in the quietness of my spirit I heard . . . forgiveness. From that moment, I began to learn the power and freedom of forgiveness.

When I realized that God promises to forgive us for our destructive thoughts, attitudes, words and behaviors, I asked for His forgiveness of all of mine. Though I knew that He would forgive me, I struggled with forgiving myself for all the ways I had brought destruction into my life and relationships.

> During my times of stillness, God urged me over and over to forgive myself.

I was so burdened by all of the unintended consequences of my harmful choices that I was unable to let go of my shame. During my times of stillness, God urged me over and over to forgive myself. He reminded me that He had already forgiven me, and that my holding on to the burden of my guilt would never set me free. I couldn't just *know* that He would forgive me; I had to *accept* that His forgiveness had already washed me clean. Eventually, I was able to truly accept the gracious gift of God's forgiveness—I finally released the burden of my guilt and forgave myself.

With this decision, I was walking toward greater freedom, but God had more to teach me about forgiveness. He showed me that accepting His forgiveness is not just about releasing my own guilt. Accepting His forgiveness requires seeking forgiveness from those we've hurt and choosing to forgive those who have hurt us. Choosing forgiveness is not always easy and does not always "feel" right, but it is a necessary choice for our freedom: "For if you forgive men when they sin against you, your heavenly Father will also forgive you. But if you do not forgive men their sins, your Father will not forgive your sins" (Matthew 6:14-15). Gradually, I chose to forgive those who had hurt me, and with a wash of healing tears, I felt the heavy burden of unforgiveness lift. I felt whole; I felt free.

> Choosing forgiveness is not always easy and does not always "feel" right, but it is a necessary choice for our freedom.

God also began to prompt me to seek forgiveness from various people I had hurt. These promptings were not all at once; in fact, some were even years after I began my journey out of my dark valley. But each time I responded in obedience to God's leading, I experienced the gift of forgiveness from that person. I encourage you to examine your heart to see if there are any remnants of unforgiveness toward those who have hurt you, or if you need to seek forgiveness from someone else. If so, press into God, and He will give you the strength and courage you need to experience forgiveness in your relationships. It is a choice worth making—forgiveness leads to freedom.

∿

As I continued to experience God's healing year after year in the deepest places of my heart, I felt empowered to freely live. I chose to be still with God daily and my life was simple and at peace. I began to use my God-given gifts to serve the people around me. I could see that God was making beauty from ashes in my life (see Isaiah 61:3). And not in spite of, but because of, that heap of ashes, He enabled me to positively impact the

> I could see that God was making beauty from ashes in my life. And not in spite of, but because of, that heap of ashes, He enabled me to positively impact the people around me.

people around me. I was discovering my God-directed purpose. It was during this exciting time in my life that I learned yet another important lesson on boundaries.

I began to feel a prompting in my heart to volunteer in my community. Just a few days later, someone called and invited me to a community meeting about an initiative I was very passionate about; I agreed to go. God was definitely calling me to get involved in this project, but once I started, other opportunities kept coming my way. I started participating in a number of different community projects, and, at first, I loved it.

People noticed all I was doing and would comment about my passion for serving God. Others would build me up with praise and then ask me to get involved in whatever projects they were involved with; I continued to say "yes" to everything. I got to the point that I felt obligated to say "yes," that somehow I would be letting others down if I wasn't involved. After all, these were all important projects in my community, and I had been given an opportunity to use my God-given gifts to serve others. I believed that involvement in these projects must be a part of my purpose, and I didn't want to miss out. I had wasted too many years while in my dark valley, and now was the opportunity to make up for lost time.

There was one problem . . . soon, I was miserable. I had gotten so overwhelmed with tasks and obligations that I had no joy or peace. I understand now that my unrest had little to do with the projects themselves—I believe that the majority were God-directed initiatives in my community—but that I was involved for all the wrong reasons. What started out as a God-directed act of obedience—to get involved in helping with some of the needs of my community—too quickly became a self or man-directed endeavor. And, it was no wonder; my busy schedule allowed little time to spend in stillness with God. I had become distracted by all the "good" things I was doing.

> My busy schedule allowed little time to spend in stillness with God. I had become distracted by all the "good" things I was doing.

Instead of spending focused time with God, I would give Him half-hearted "high fives"—five minutes here, five minutes there—that provided no opportunity for me to rest in His presence and hear His direction. I thought that God would somehow excuse me from resting in His presence since I was serving His people. What I neglected to understand was that I could not effectively serve His people without spending focused time in His presence. Only then would I be able to discern the specific tasks that God had for me, and the specific people He desired me to serve. Only then could I receive His direction for the next step on my journey.

> I could not effectively serve His people without spending focused time in His presence.

When I realized that I had turned onto a detour, I cried out to God to help me. Just a short time after taking the problem to God, something amazing happened. A pastor friend of mine showed up at my front door and said he felt led to bring some CDs to me. I had never talked to him about my situation, but I knew God heard my cry and directed him to bring me exactly what I needed. I listened to them immediately and began taking notes. I clearly heard the nugget of God's wisdom that I needed to re-direct me back onto God's path—I had been following man's plan for my life instead of God's. That was why I was so overwhelmed.

> I had been following man's plan for my life instead of God's. That was why I was so overwhelmed.

As I listened to these CDs and got still in God's presence again, He reminded me that each person has a unique God-directed purpose with specific tasks to complete (see Ephesians 2:10). No one person is called to address all of the needs around us. God spoke to my heart saying, "The right hand and the left hand of the body of Christ look similar, but is the right hand supposed to do the left hand's duty?"

He said, "Abby, I didn't call you to do all the tasks that you are involved in; you have allowed man to distract you. You are doing things that are not bad, but they are not what I called *you* to do. My yolk is light; you are carrying way too much. I have actually called others to do some of the jobs that you are doing. Until you remove yourself from these positions, you are preventing them from receiving the blessing of doing this work. You are the right hand trying to serve in the left hand's position" (see Romans 12:4-8, 1 Corinthians 12:12-31).

God also impressed on me the importance of discerning where He actually desired me to serve when being approached about new opportunities. During this time, several people succeeded in convincing me to serve in roles by telling me that God told them I was the person for the job. I know now that simply taking their word for it was not wise.

As I cried out to Him for relief from my busyness, God assured me, "I will place my intention for you on *your* heart first. Then, I will use other people or signs to confirm it. I called you to the first project, but then you got excited and left me. Little by little you allowed yourself to get distracted by your pride and your desire to please others over your desire to please me. You allowed your time with me to be destroyed, therefore taking your peace and joy."

He also made me realize how little time I had actually been spending in His presence. In the quietness of my heart, I heard Him say, "You began giving me "high fives," instead of taking time to be still in my presence, which diminished your ability to hear what I was saying to you. I would never

> You can't be a light to the world when the light in you is not visible anymore.

call you to do so much that it takes your joy. You can't be a light to the world when the light in you is not visible anymore.

"Seek me continually. Don't let your pride and ego get in the way, and don't make decisions based on your emotions. When you feel pressured, obligated or guilted into doing something, take a moment to reflect. Most of the time, these are wrong motivations for getting involved, no matter how worthwhile a cause it may be. Learn to seek me first in all that you do. Learn to say "no" and to resist anything that distracts you from what I am calling you to do. Remember, I will always place it on your heart first, and then you will get a confirmation to move forward."

I am so thankful that God so clearly re-directed my path. Over the next few weeks, I began to recognize and remove myself from the things—even the good and worthwhile things—that were not God-directed in my life. I re-committed myself to diligently seeking His direction, working to set aside my

> I began to recognize and remove myself from the things—even the good and worthwhile things—that were not God-directed in my life.

pride and misguided desire to please others.

Now, when someone gives me an opportunity to serve in some way, I take time to seek God's will on the matter. I say "yes" only if God has prompted my spirit toward it. If I am not feeling led to do it, I gently and confidently decline and thank them for thinking of me. God knows exactly what I am called to do, and I would much rather be obedient to Him than to only please myself or others.

Does your life feel light or heavy right now? Is it chaotic or simple? Do you need to remove yourself from things that you know are distracting you and are taking your peace and joy?

If you are overwhelmed and busy all the time, stop. Take time to seek God's direction. Ask God to make

> We have to be willing to rest in His presence long enough to hear His voice, and then listen to and obey His direction.

clear where you are off track and to give you the wisdom and courage to remove yourself from the things that have gotten you off of God's path. Remember, His yolk is light.

God is faithful to lead us and guide us, but He will not force Himself on us. We have to be willing to rest in His presence long enough to hear His voice, and then listen to and obey His direction. Only then will we be able to set the God-directed boundaries that help us to climb unhindered out of our dark valleys, freeing us to live the unique and purposeful lives that God has planned for us.

16

Finding Balanced Simplicity

Finding balance and simplicity in life has become a much-discussed pursuit in our modern culture. Most of us have probably at some point felt the weight of living imbalanced, complex lives. Some of us, perceiving the potential harm in living this way, may have actually spent time and energy battling against our chaotic lifestyles. We may have been able to change certain behaviors that helped simplify things or motivate us for a time.

But, how many of us have achieved lasting freedom from the pressure to do more, to be more? What about freedom from the worldly things that control us or distract us from our God-given purposes? I would guess not many of us have found this freedom.

Ironically, it is fairly easy for us to sense when our lives are out of balance, but we cannot seem to live consistently balanced lives. Perhaps this is because we tend to fail miserably in our ability to identify and root out the beliefs and attitudes which feed our chaotic living. In order to live lives of balanced simplicity we have to address those imbalanced roots.

> We tend to fail miserably in our ability to identify and root out the beliefs and attitudes which feed our chaotic living.

To identify the make-up of our imbalanced roots, we must take time to evaluate our priorities. A lack of God-directed priorities will allow those imbalanced roots to thrive, bringing chaos to our lives. However,

> Allowing God to direct our priorities will bring balance, simplicity and peace to our lives.

allowing God to direct our priorities will bring balance, simplicity and peace to our lives.

From the moment God pursued me in the midst of my chaotic life, He began to shift my perspective and to realign my focus—the priority of my life from that day forward was to rest in His presence, to practice stillness with Him. This was, and continues to be, the foundation of my healing and my freedom to live.

At the beginning of my journey, my imbalanced roots produced chaos in virtually every aspect of my life. I was out of balance spiritually, physically, mentally, nutritionally, financially and relationally; I was trapped in my dark valley. During my practice of stillness, God helped me to see that my misaligned priorities had made it easy for me to be controlled by or, at a minimum, distracted by something other than God's priorities for my life.

In the midst of my chaotic living, my priority was myself—what I wanted to do, and when I wanted to do it. I did not consider how my lifestyle affected anyone else, or that my self-destructive choices were actually a form of selfishness. Putting priority on self prevented me from living the life of service that I now know God designs for each of us. As God revealed more of Himself to me, I knew that I wanted to realign my priorities to His and balance my life.

Some areas of imbalance in my life were easy to spot, such as my addictions. But, I also began to recognize my imbalanced roots when God prompted me to evaluate the way I was spending my time. My life was full of inconsistencies. I would spend countless hours playing on the computer and watching television, yet I would complain that I didn't have enough time to do the things I needed, or even wanted, to do.

I would typically react to my time-wasting in one of two ways: Either I would feel the great pressure and stress that usually result from poor time management (or, perhaps, poor priority management). Or, I would feel bored, with little motivation to do anything to change the course of my future. I was out of balance.

I also became aware of how often I complained of being broke, yet I was constantly shopping and spending money on things I thought I had to have. I didn't feel well physically, yet I didn't take the time to evaluate the negative effects of the food and drink I was putting into my body. I was out of balance.

Do you recognize areas in your life that are out of balance? What might these imbalances show you about what your priorities are? Are you willing to re-align your priorities in order to find freedom from chaotic living?

Bringing your life into balance requires you to make changes. Lasting freedom comes when we commit to making changes that line up with God's priorities for our lives. Though He has unique, specific purposes for each person, God's desire for all of us is to love Him and spend time knowing Him. When asked, Jesus said that the "first and greatest commandment" is to "love the Lord your God with all your heart and with all your soul and with all your mind" (Matthew 22:38,37).

> Though He has unique, specific purposes for each person, God's desire for all of us is to love Him and spend time knowing Him.

God's desire in this is not merely that we would know about Him, but that our lives would be transformed because of Him. Simply put, our life-transforming encounters with God bring our lives into balance. It is during our time with Him that we receive wisdom and direction as to how to live lives that are balanced according to His priorities. Embracing this lifestyle allows us to freely live the lives God has planned for us.

So, what are God's priorities beyond us being in a loving relationship with Him? Throughout Scripture, we see God's heart for people and personal relationships over tasks or material possessions. Jesus said that the second greatest commandment is like the first: "love your neighbor as yourself" (Matthew 22:39). Loving God and loving others should be our guiding principles when determining the priorities for our own lives. Serving people—namely our spouse (if we are married), followed by our children, other family members, friends and anyone else God directs you to serve—should take priority over our careers and other tasks or activities.

Making people our priority does not mean that diligent work or leisure activities are not legitimate. Nor does it mean that we neglect care for ourselves physically, spiritually or emotionally. It does mean, however, that we are willing to set aside our tasks, possessions or

> Being able to discern God's priorities for each day of your life is developed by resting in His presence. This is how we learn to practice balanced simplicity.

ambitions whenever the people in our lives need our service. Being able to discern God's priorities for each day of your life is developed by resting in His presence. This is how we learn to practice balanced simplicity.

Misplaced priorities keep us trapped in our chaotic lifestyles. In this place, we suffer from frustration, feeling overwhelmed, emotional or physical pain and broken relationships, to name a few. It's time to be honest. You have twenty-four hours in every day. How are you using your time? Are you putting people above your career, tasks and possessions—or the other way around?

During my journey, I was inspired to consider the way I spent my time by the story of a pastor who was experiencing great pain and stress as a result of putting his career over his family. He recognized his misplaced priorities and committed to changing the focus of his life. Are you? I accepted the challenge to straighten out my priorities, and I have experienced God's rich blessings—namely peace, joy and restored relationships—as a result.

> I accepted the challenge to straighten out my priorities, and I have experienced God's rich blessings—namely peace, joy and restored relationships.

I live out my priority realignment in several practical ways. Above all, I continue to practice stillness with God on a daily basis. This is my life-force, the place I receive direction for each day. From this place, I also now protect and care for important relationships.

Before, my relationship with my husband was a total mess; we were two strangers living in the same house. Our words were not full of love, but of distrust, jealousy, anger, fear and control. I did not respect my husband's role as the leader of our family, so I used fear and manipulation to control him, but then sabotaged any attempt he made to improve things. We both used partying to try to escape our problems, which, of course, made things worse.

As I realigned my priorities, God completely transformed our marriage. He empowered us with perseverance, patience, forgiveness and unconditional love. He restored trust and open communication. Though we still have our ups and downs, we are quick to communicate, forgive and move forward in our relationship. We are a true testament of God's power to save a marriage that was headed for complete destruction. Now, we both prioritize our marriage over any other human relationship. We set aside dedicated time each week for a date night so that we have built-in time to connect and care for our relationship. Knowing that both of us make the other a priority has done amazing things for our marriage.

I have also changed the way I prioritize my extended family. In the past, my relationship with my parents and other family members was virtually non-existent. I rarely talked with them on the phone, and would go out of my way to be busy when they came for a visit. I took no responsibility for myself in this, blaming them for all of the problems.

But, as I recognized my misplaced priorities, God empowered me to make changes in these relationships as well. Now, I have re-opened positive, encouraging communication between us, and we talk on the phone several times a week. When they come for a visit, I schedule time off of work so that I can focus on them. My family members have taken notice, and our relationships have strengthened because of it.

I hope to continue to live out my priority realignment as a parent. My husband and I desire to keep our marriage as the central human relationship in our family and for our relationships with God to remain supreme. We also desire to prevent our careers from coming before our family. We want to preserve enough energy for our family that we can spend time playing together, helping with homework and enjoying regular family dinners together. I want to be present in the life of my family, remembered as someone who was available to meet their needs, not as a person preoccupied with work.

I know that this will be a challenge. The balanced life is not easily maintained without constant evaluation of our priorities and a willingness to make adjustments when things fall out of balance. We must be intentional about the way we prioritize our lives; a lack of intentionality leads only to unbalanced living. Thankfully, God can help us identify anything that

> The balanced life is not easily maintained without constant evaluation of our priorities and a willingness to make adjustments when things fall out of balance.

does not line up with His priorities as we cry out to Him: "Search me, O God, and know my heart; test me and know my anxious thoughts. See if there is any offensive way in me, and lead me in the way everlasting" (Psalm 139: 23-24).

Allowing God to search the inner places of our hearts and minds will tip us off to the imbalances that distract our living. We must be on guard. The world is full of distractions that, if not seen for what they are, keep our minds and hearts controlled by them instead of by God. Distractions can cause us to be too busy or too bored. Both of these states cause us to miss opportunities to freely live the lives that God has planned for us.

> The world is full of distractions that, if not seen for what they are, keep our minds and hearts controlled by them instead of by God.

Are you too busy or too bored? When we are busy, we are certainly distracted. The very word *busy* feels like a curse. It evokes overwhelming, negative feelings in us because we have all experienced the chaos of busy. Being B-U-S-Y can be thought of as Being Under Satan's Yolk. Under this influence, we typically neglect resting in God's presence and are often distracted from what He is calling us to do. When I hear people say they are too busy, I encourage them to seek God's direction on how to structure their time. God calls us to be active servants, but He does not desire us to be so active that we feel chaotic and lose our joy.

When we are living the lives that God has called us to, we may have much to accomplish, but it will be accompanied by peace, strength and a sense of purpose. Because of this, I encourage people to remove the word *busy* from their vocabulary and replace it with *blessed* instead. We are indeed blessed that God chooses us to be active participants in fulfilling His purposes in our lives and the lives of those around us.

> We are indeed blessed that God chooses us to be active participants in fulfilling His purposes in our lives and the lives of those around us.

But, what if we are bored? If you feel unmotivated, stuck in your situation or like you are just going through the motions of day to day living, you may also be distracted. In this case, you may not feel busy enough, so you waste time on things that lack effective purpose.

Activities like watching television, playing video games, surfing the Internet and even reading are just a few examples of things that can be distractions that keep us off the course that God has set for us.

The things that tempt us to be busy, as well as those that encourage our boredom, all have the potential not just to distract us, but to control us. Most of these things are not harmful—some are even helpful—to us in moderation, but it is difficult to keep them in check. Even too much of a good thing can hurt you. We make idols of these things at times without even realizing it.

Consider where you put most of your time and energy, what you spend most of your time thinking about; this is most likely what controls you. If you desire material wealth, power or success, your job may control you. If you feel you have to portray a certain physical image, shopping or the pursuit of beauty can control you. There are countless other examples to consider.

A simple way to determine if you are out of balance, and therefore being controlled by something, is to go without it for a while. Obviously, I am not suggesting that you quit your job, but consider not working all the extra hours, or don't take work home with you for a couple of weeks. Remove yourself from a few activities. Do a media-fast where you turn off the television, cell phone, computer, MP3 player and radio for a few days. Stop shopping. Stop golfing. Stop drinking or eating unhealthy foods. Stop whatever it is that is wasting all of your time. By removing these things, you will probably be able to tell if it controls you.

I encourage you to ask God to reveal if your current priorities are causing your life to be out of balance. When He shows you, ask Him to help you realign them so that you can find a balance where you can enjoy things in life without being controlled by them. Ask Him to give you the strength and discipline needed to climb out of your chaotic lifestyle—whether you are busy or bored—in order to gain peace, simplicity and a sense of purposeful living.

God has always been faithful to guide and direct me out of my dark valley, but I had to commit to take action and make the changes necessary to balance my life. As I yield to Him, He removes my desires for the things that were causing my life

> God has always been faithful to guide and direct me out of my dark valley, but I had to commit to take action and make the changes necessary to balance my life.

to be out of balance; now I have complete freedom to live. I no longer struggle with addictions. I don't feel the constant need to seek approval from others, and I have learned to say "no" to requests from people when I don't feel led to participate.

The things of this world do not control me as they once did. I live a life of balanced simplicity, and I am free to live the life God has planned for me. God desires to empower you to live the life He has planned for you. As you rest in His presence, surrender to Him the misplaced priorities and things that distract or control you. Begin moving forward and trust that God will equip you with everything you need to live a life of balanced simplicity.

17

Living With Passion and Purpose

As God continued to heal me from chaotic living, my priorities began to change. I set new boundaries to support my healing and learned to practice balanced simplicity in living. Additionally, I noticed that some of my passions—the things that inspired me—started to change.

As I surrendered to God's leading, I realized that He was redirecting my career. Though the process of changing careers was one of the most challenging periods in my life, I am so thankful that I followed God's leading. Now, I get to live out my passion in my job. God has matched my passion with my paycheck.

A couple of years into my healing journey, I began to feel unsettled in my job as a retail manager. I did not hate my job and was good at it, but I felt that something was missing. It had solely become a means to make money; I didn't feel at all inspired by or purposeful in my work.

As I sought God, I knew He was leading me in a new direction—to go to massage therapy school. At first I was fearful and resisted because I had no idea how I could go back to school while still managing the retail store. After all, there are only so many hours in a day, right? For a couple of months, I went back and forth on the idea, but each time I decided there was just no way I would be able to work and go to school full time.

However, despite my repeated refusals, I had no peace about my decision. There was a constant stirring in my spirit that nudged me forward. As I surrendered to God's leading, He assured me that though I was not able to take on the demands of working full-time and going to school full-time, He was. By His power, He would equip me to handle this change that He was asking me to make, "for I can do everything through Christ, who gives me strength" (Philippians 4:13 (NLT)). I talked to my husband, and he agreed that I should do it. After fighting God's leading for all those months, I finally said yes.

> By His power, He would equip me to handle this change that He was asking me to make.

Before I could move forward, I had to do several things that I knew would be difficult and uncomfortable for me. Though I knew that this career change was God's leading, there were several factors that seemed to stand firmly in the way. One could have argued that there were just too many obstacles, too many unknowns, to take this leap of faith. But, I knew that if God had directed this, He would knock down anything standing in the way. I had to continue to trust Him for each next step.

> I knew that if God had directed this, He would knock down anything standing in the way.

The first uncertainty was how my boss, and friend of four years, would react to the news of me going back to school so that I could pursue a different career. I had no idea if he would even allow me to go to school and continue to work as his manager. He was not on-board at first, but after a long and intense discussion, he agreed to the arrangement as long as attending school did not interfere with my ability to perform my job duties. Obstacle one was toppled.

The next thing I had to do was to figure out how to fund my schooling. Since I already had a Bachelor's degree, I wasn't eligible for many grants, and the federal loan I qualified for would only cover a portion of the cost of tuition. I felt God directing me to ask my father for a loan. My father had always enjoyed being able to help his children in times of need, but I was not very close to him at that time, so I was unsure how he would react to my request. I had not reached out to him in years; this was definitely a risk.

I swallowed my pride and called to ask if he would be willing to help me pay for my schooling. Without hesitation, my dad agreed to help me and loaned me several thousand dollars, which I have since been able to repay in full. Asking my father for help not only provided my financial need, but was a big step in the right direction for healing in our relationship. Obstacle two was toppled, and I received the added blessing of the beginning of a restored relationship with my father. The decision to change careers was validated yet again.

The final hurdle was to figure out how in the world I was going to work an average of 50 hours a week, drive an hour each way to attend school 20–25 hours a week and still find time to study on top of that. Were there really enough hours in the day? Was this actually possible? I was very doubtful when I first wrote out my schedule. I had every hour of every day tied up with work, school, studying and sleep. There was no room for anything else.

I was concerned that this pace of life would interfere with my practice of stillness with God. And, I knew that taking my focus off of Him would have chaotic results. But, I found time with God while driving to and from school; this time-eating commute was actually vital to maintaining my connection with God, and therefore, key to my ability to accomplish all that He was asking me to do.

As I presented myself before Him those two hours each day in the car, He strengthened and refreshed me. He walked me through these months seeming to stretch my time and helped me remain connected with my husband despite our limited time together. God removed all of the major obstacles to making a career change; I then had to continue to respond to His leading.

I started massage school in March of 2005 and graduated with a 4.0 in November of that same year. I never would have imagined that I could do all that I did that year and still manage to come out on top. I grew so much and discovered what I believe is my lifelong passion and purpose—to help people find whole healing of spirit, mind and body—so that they can freely live the lives God is calling them to live.

I felt so inspired and empowered that I started my own business, Healing Naturally, shortly after graduation. I had no clients, and I was leaving a job that paid me a comfortable salary. I had no idea how it was going to work out, but I knew that God was directing me to do it.

> I knew nothing was impossible that God was directing.

Having a successful business would no doubt require hard work and focus, but after God empowered me to accomplish what He had while I was in massage school, I knew nothing was impossible that God was directing.

God opened all the right doors, provided the finances and blessed my business with lots of clients. I share this with you because I am living proof that God can match our passions with our paychecks. I feel inspired every day by what God has called me to do. I know without a doubt that I am on the right path. I have now been in business for over five years and God continues to open new doors and amazing opportunities for me to help people on their journeys to whole healing. This is my passion.

Do you feel inspired by your work? Do you feel a sense of purpose in your job? Do your passions line up with the way you spend your time? Are you willing to follow God's leading if He is prompting you to pursue something different?

Take a moment to consider whether your life is characterized by passion and purpose, or if you are just going through the motions. It is easy to settle into a routine. Most of the time routines feel familiar, comfortable and secure. There is nothing wrong with routines unless maintaining them overrides our willingness to follow God's leading in a different direction.

> There is nothing wrong with routines unless maintaining them overrides our willingness to follow God's leading in a different direction.

When we feel unable or are unwilling to change our routines, we are in a rut. When we are in this place, our lives are usually lived without passion and purpose. We should not be satisfied with life like this; God desires something more fulfilling for each of our lives.

Do not miss the opportunity to live out your God-given passion and purpose. It is important to note that living this way is not only achieved by matching your passion with your paycheck. You may not be pursuing a paid career outside of the home, but you can still live a life of passion and purpose in other ways, such as in your personal relationships or through volunteer service. Also, remember that it is never too late in life to discover (or re-discover) your passion and to live it out in this phase of your life.

What is your passion? What is your purpose? You may have been in a rut for so long that you are unable to identify either in your life. Or, you may sense what they are, but you feel unable to move in their direction. Undoubtedly, you were designed for something special. Do not let yourself stay in the rut.

> Undoubtedly, you were designed for something special. Do not let yourself stay in the rut.

God may not call you to change careers, but He will certainly help you to change your perspective. Be still with God, and allow Him to reveal your passions and what He created you to do. Resist the temptation to be ruled by fear and doubt. Listen to His guidance, and take the next step. If I would have given into my fears and doubts when faced with the decision to leave my comfortable job for an uncertain career, I would have strayed off the path God had in store for me. And, I would have missed out on the joy of living out my passion at work and in life.

God kept nudging me forward, but it was up to me to actively respond to His leading and to trust Him to direct me to each next step. It took a lot of faith, trust, courage, determination, discipline and focus to do what God was calling me to do. Thankfully, as I surrendered to Him, He equipped me to accomplish all that He asked me to do. This was as true for this particular situation in my life as it is for navigating my life today.

Continuing to live with passion and purpose requires practicing my faith and trust in Him to do what He calls me to do each day. I have to remain focused on living intentionally and continue to seek God daily, but I know that He will equip me step by step for all He calls me to do. He will also equip you as you seek Him.

> Continuing to live with passion and purpose requires practicing my faith and trust in Him to do what He calls me to do each day.

Be encouraged—the journey, even with its apparent uncertainty, is worth it. When we choose to walk by faith, trusting that God will guide us every step of the way, we will begin to freely live with passion and purpose.

18

Be Love and Give Love

A passion that God desires to stir in all of His children is the passion to live a life of love and service to others. If we are honest, we can probably admit that a passion for others—as opposed to a passion for ourselves—is not our natural state of mind.

But remember, as God's children, we are not called to live enslaved to ourselves, but rather to live freed from self-focus. We are called to live lives that are characterized by love. We cannot consistently live like this on our own strength and discipline; it is impossible. But, we can live more like this as we are transformed by God, for He is love (see 1 John 4:8).

But, what does living a life of "love" mean? Looking toward our culture for a definition of "love" could be confusing, and maybe even unsettling. However, looking at the Bible's definition of love is more clearly defined. It gives us a picture not of a feeling that comes and goes, but of a set of defined choices about how to live in relation to others.

It is also a description of God's character: "Love is patient, love is kind. It does not envy, it does not boast, it is not proud. It is not rude, it is not self seeking, it is not easily angered, it keeps no record of wrongs. Love does not delight in evil, but rejoices with the truth. It always protects, always trusts, always hopes, always perseveres.

> As we are transformed by God, His love will begin to flow out of us, enabling us to be love to those around us.

Love never fails" (1 Corinthians 13:4-8). Living a life of love like this requires us to allow God's love to overtake our hearts and minds, and even then we will never perfectly love all of the time. But, as we are transformed by God, His love will begin to flow out of us, enabling us to be love to those around us.

At times, we get it all backwards; we may try to be love to others when we have not taken the time to rest in God's presence and fill up on His love. Without it, we may be full of sorrow, self-pity, bitterness, anger, fear, judgment or self-focus. We are so trapped in our dark valleys that even if we want to extend love to others, we find it difficult to actually follow through.

Or, we may appear to love and serve others, but a closer examination of our hearts reveals misplaced motivations. Doing something with self-serving motivation, even something that appears loving, is *not* biblical love. Think about it. Not inviting God to fill us with His love leaves us completely empty and incapable of extending His love to others. The good news is that God's love is unlimited and is always available to us; it is up to us to allow Him to fill us with it (paraphrase of Ephesians 3:17-19).

Can you sense when you have not allowed God's love to fill you up? Are you willing to take time to rest in God's presence so that you can tap into His power to be love?

Recognizing when we have neglected to allow God's love to fill us is the first step in learning to practice a life of love. When I feel empty, tired, stressed or short-tempered, I have learned to admit that I am living on my own strength—and am failing miserably. I am reminded that I need God to refill my love tank so that I can be love to those around me.

Before I have a chance to react in an unloving way, I choose to take a few minutes to turn my focus back to God. I make a conscious decision to let it all go and just breathe, and He always fills me right back up. It really is that simple. We can choose to stop, refocus and allow God to transform our perspective on our circumstances. Or, we can choose the destructive path where we hurt others and ourselves.

> We can choose to stop, refocus and allow God to transform our perspective on our circumstances.

Too often we choose to live on our own strength, letting our tanks get lower and lower, until there is nothing left. When we are depleted, we often feel out of control and may begin to act out, saying things we later regret. Or, we may start to respond to others out of fear or other negative thought or behavior patterns. On this path, we are not being love to those around us.

I desire for people to see the love of God flowing in and through me. I hope that when someone looks at my life, he or she will see Jesus and be greatly affected by His love in me. However, in order to be an expression of God's love, I have to continually accept and allow His love to take over my life; I have to ensure that my love tank is full.

> In order to be an expression of God's love, I have to continually accept and allow His love to take over my life; I have to ensure that my love tank is full.

When it is, God's love, joy, peace, patience, kindness, goodness, faithfulness, gentleness and self-control will flow out of me. But, if my love tank is empty, or even running low, then the ugly motivations of my heart will show themselves. My life will not be characterized by love, but by bitterness, judgment, anger, fear, jealously, greed, lust, pride or selfishness—to name just a few.

What flows out of you? Do people see God's love when they look at your life? Or, do they see a person who is only living for self?

Take time to evaluate your life in relation to the biblical definition of love in 1 Corinthians 13. Are you patient and kind? Do you resist the temptation to envy, to boast, to be proud? Do you turn from being rude, self-seeking, and easily angered? Are you tempted to keep record of wrongs? Do you delight in evil or rejoice with the truth? Do you protect, trust, hope and persevere in relationships? Or, do you fail others?

This can be a pretty convicting exercise, but one that is not intended to condemn you or make you feel guilty. Allow it to make you aware of the areas of your life that you are not living in love, areas that God still wishes to refine in you. In addition to this exercise, you may consider asking someone you trust to help you evaluate your life.

Sometimes we are unable to see the areas of our lives that need attention, even when they are obvious to others. Asking someone to help you see areas where you are not demonstrating God's love requires us to humble ourselves and to prepare ourselves to hear things we may not want to hear. Though this can be difficult, great growth can come from learning to accept hard truths. Allow what you find to motivate you to keep climbing toward God and allow Him to transform you.

> When we pay attention to keeping our love tanks full, God transforms us so that we will freely live in love and service to others.

When we pay attention to keeping our love tanks full, God transforms us so that we will freely live in love and service to others. We will begin to live out the Golden Rule—treating others the way we want to be treated—with love and respect. Jesus commands us to live by this principle: "So in everything, do to others what you would have them do to you, for this sums up the Law and the Prophets" (Matthew 7:12).

When we live by this principle, we extend God's love to those around us. We are motivated not by what we can potentially gain—such as recognition, encouragement, praise or love—from treating others well. Rather, we are compelled to live out the Golden Rule because, by His love, God has transformed us. Once we have been changed by God's love, we will offer it to others by the way we live.

We also must know that living out God's love does not exempt us from mistreatment from others. Even when we treat others with love and respect, there will still be times that we are mistreated, or even actively persecuted, by others. This does not give us license to treat them badly in return.

Notice that Jesus does *not* say, "Treat others the way they treat you." He holds us to a higher standard, but one that He also held to Himself. Jesus was ridiculed, mocked, insulted, accused of blasphemy and was ultimately put to death, but He did not take revenge. As He was crucified, He displayed love even for his executioners with His plea to God: "Father, forgive them, for they do not know what they are doing" (Luke 23:34). Jesus chose to extend love even in his darkest hour; we have the same choice.

The next time you are mistreated, take time to draw on God's love so that you can be empowered to love and forgive that person. This is not easy, as it sometimes requires us to swallow our wounded pride or set aside our desire to seek revenge. Loving those who mistreat us does not excuse their bad behavior, nor does it mean that we ignore the very real pain caused by their treatment of us. But consider that God is giving you an opportunity to extend love and forgiveness to someone who may be deeply hurting. Often, someone's mistreatment of you is primarily an overflow of his or her inner pain and insecurity, and actually has little to do with you. That said, take time to search your heart and ask God to reveal anything that you have said or done to contribute to the conflict. Paying close attention and attending to these areas of our own lives is an important part of freeing ourselves to love those who mistreat us.

Living a life of love and service to others does not come naturally to us; it requires a commitment to rest daily in God's presence and a willingness to surrender to His plans and purposes for all circumstances in our lives. Do not be so focused on yourself that you miss the opportunity God has given you to extend His love to another, even someone who is difficult to love.

~

Living lives of love requires self-sacrifice. If we are not freely giving our time, energy, talents and resources to the service of others, we are not living lives characterized by biblical love. Though God calls each person to serve in a unique way, His call for all of us is the same—to extend His love and grace to others through service: "Each one should use whatever gift he has received to serve others, faithfully administering God's grace in its various forms. If anyone speaks, he should do it as one speaking the very words of God. If anyone serves, he should do it with the strength God provides, so that in all things God may be praised through Jesus Christ. To him be the glory and the power forever and ever" (1Peter 4:10-11). This is what it means to be love.

> Though God calls each person to serve in a unique way, His call for all of us is the same—to extend His love and grace to others through service.

How much of your time, energy, talents and resources do you unselfishly give to serve others? Are you open to letting God show you where He wants to use you to serve someone in need? Do you believe that He will equip you for whatever service He is asking of you?

At one point in my life, I only served myself. My life was all about me and what I could get out of it. I never unselfishly gave of my time, energy, talents and resources, and I certainly wasn't looking for opportunities to serve others. If I did do something for someone, it was almost always selfishly motivated—I expected something in return.

At the time, I did not realize how self-centered my life was; if you live like I did, you may not realize it either. But, the more time I spent resting in God's presence and allowing His love to fill me, the more obvious my selfishness became. I did not want to live like that anymore. Over time, God changed my heart, and I even began praying for opportunities to serve others. I often prayed that He would bless me with the ability to do a special favor for someone, and every single time God provided me with the opportunity to do just that. I began to experience the joy in unselfishly serving others, even when it stretched me.

> I began to experience the joy in unselfishly serving others, even when it stretched me.

Seeing the ways God uses me to meet the specific needs of people around me blesses my heart and encourages me to keep serving. God doesn't always prompt me to do easy, pleasant favors, but I always try to do them joyfully, expecting nothing in return. Serving others has also helped me re-focus my perspective and to be more thankful for my life.

I have learned to trust that if God is directing me to give in some way—whether of my time, energy, talents or financial resources—He is faithful to provide all that I need. My husband and I have particularly experienced growth in the area of trusting God with our finances. Now, if God places it on our hearts to give money to someone or something— even if we think we cannot afford it—we give in faith, trusting Him for our provision. At different points in our lives, we have been stretched to give more than we thought we could afford, but God has always taken care of us as we chose to trust Him. I challenge you to trust Him to do whatever it is He is prompting you to do. He is faithful.

~

So, what *is* He prompting you to do? What changes does He want you to make so that you will be free to live? Take time to be still in His presence, and allow His love to fill you. Do not settle for a life lived with even one toe stuck in your dark valley. God desires to deliver you, to restore you, to make

> Do not settle for a life lived with even one toe stuck in your dark valley.

you whole. He is "mighty to save. He will take great delight in you, He will quiet you with His love, He will rejoice over you with singing" (Zephaniah 3:17). God is ready and waiting "to strengthen those whose hearts are fully committed to him" (2 Chronicles 16:9). Now is the time. Turn toward His light. Surrender to His love and power to equip you for service, and climb out of the chaos.

We are all called to freely live in love and service to others, but we cannot do this from the darkness. We must keep moving toward the light. Only then will we freely live out the unique plan and purpose that God has designed for each one of us. We cannot carry out our call to serve others on our own strength, but we can certainly rely on His. Give your life away to be transformed by God, and then freely live out of His love. This is the greatest calling of all. Be Love. Give Love.

RECOGNIZING GOD

I could probably write another entire book solely about the amazing ways that God has made Himself known to me over the course of my journey. I often say my life is like having a front row seat to the best show in town. When you walk with God on a daily basis and seek Him continually, you will see amazing things that are evidence of His activity in your life.

My journey has been full of these instances. I am not one of God's "special" children who gets extra blessings that are not available to everyone else. You are just as special to Him as I am, and He delights in blessing you and showing you His love. He loves each one of His children; the difference is that not all of us open our eyes to see Him.

> He loves each one of His children; the difference is that not all of us open our eyes to see Him.

Two people can look at the same image, person or situation and see two entirely different things. Consider the optical illusion that seems to consist only of dots, but when you stare at the dots long enough, a picture appears. When you first look at one of those illusions, you only see dots—no picture. Then your friend next to you may say, "I see it, I see the picture—it's a sailboat." You may think, *there is no way there is a sailboat in the middle of this mess; all I see is dots*. So you try harder and persevere because you reason that if your friend saw it, then you should be able to see it too. After several minutes of trying, you find yourself getting frustrated; your eyes start to hurt, and you want to give up.

You start believing that you will never see the sailboat. You envy your friend's delight in finding it in the midst of the mess of dots. In your weariness, you take a deep breath, relax and stare a while longer because you are determined to see the sailboat you know is there. You stay focused, and then, out of nowhere and when you least expect it, the sailboat appears in the midst of all the dots. You are overtaken with joy because you finally see it. Each time you go back to that image it becomes easier and easier to see it. And eventually, the dots no longer cloud the picture; all you see is the sailboat.

So, are you focused on the dots in your life or on the sailboat? The dots represent the things that contribute to your chaotic life. The dots could be anxiety, constant worrying, anger, frustration, depression, judgment, control issues, sickness, relationship problems, bad circumstances, financial issues, negative attitudes, negative thoughts and words, a death in the family or addictions, to name just a few.

> God was there all along, but the chaos, at first, hid Him from your view. But now that you have seen Him, you recognize Him every time.

The sailboat emerges as the steady, peaceful presence in the midst of the chaos; the sailboat is God. He was there all along, but the chaos, at first, hid Him from your view. But now that you have seen Him, you recognize Him every time.

Commit to looking for Him in everything, all the time. As His children, God says He will never leave us or forsake us (see Deuteronomy 31:6), so that means He is everywhere that we are, and He is for us. Ask Him to reveal Himself to you, and He will amaze you. Keep your eyes open, waiting to receive evidence of His majesty, sovereignty, faithfulness, goodness, love and care for you.

These are gifts God designs specifically for you in the same way a father would give his child a special gift just to say, "I love you." I have started recording God's special gifts to me in my journal so that I can easily recall them in times of uncertainty, doubt and struggle. Having them written down allows me to go back and reflect on how faithful and loving He has been to me in the past. This remembrance gives me hope for His care for me in my present circumstances and in my future.

The following are just a few examples of the many ways God has revealed His character to me. These special gifts are evidence of God's presence in my life:

God as Creator

I one time saw a giant butterfly, the kind that is several inches tall. I really wanted to see one again, so I decided to ask God if He would allow me to see one. Just a few hours later, I found one sitting on my screen door. Butterflies are my favorite little creation from God, and He knew that it would touch my heart and bring me great joy. It was a special gift from God just to say, "I love you, Abby."

I view the sky as God's canvas and imagine Him painting me a special little picture as I am delighting in Him. One time I was sitting outside looking up at the sky, and He allowed me to see a giant happy face in the clouds. This was just another special gift from God to say I am here, and I love you.

God as Healer

I was in a season in my massage career where I was imagining what it would be like to give Jesus one of my nurturing massages. When my clients would come in for a massage, I would close my eyes and imagine I was massaging Jesus. The love that was poured out during this time was amazing for me and for my clients.

Then, I had a client come in who actually played the part of Jesus in one of the shows in my town. I didn't think much of it until he turned over onto his stomach and began to explain all the markings on his back. In order to make his body look like Jesus' beaten body for the show, the makeup artist used dye to put whip markings along his back which actually stained his skin. It was quite a sight to see. I was immediately humbled and was reminded of the pain and suffering Jesus endured when He died on the cross for me.

I began to massage my client's back, and the most amazing thing happened. As I imagined I was massaging Jesus' back, I allowed God's pure, healing love to flow through me and into my client. As I continued to massage, the stains on his back slowly disappeared.

I was so touched by the experience that it was hard for me to hold back my tears. It was as if God, through me, was actually healing Jesus' back from the stripes He bore for you and me. In that moment, God spoke to me and told me that amazing healing comes when things are done in love, not just in massaging, but in all that I do. I know that God is love and that great healing power comes from His love. I believe He allowed me to have this experience to remind me of His great healing love for me and those around me.

God as Comforter

Often when I am hurting, one of my friends or family members will send me a text, call or just show up at my door because God put me on their hearts. Sometimes they offer words of encouragement, prayer or just a shoulder to cry on. That is God taking care of me because He loves me and knows when I am in pain.

God as Love

One day I was deeply confused about some things, so I took time out for a walk in nature. As I was walking around enjoying the beauty all around me, I asked God to reveal Himself to me. I began talking to Him and told Him I wanted to see Him. I just needed to experience Him in a tangible way.

As I continued to walk around, I had a sudden urge to use the restroom. As I changed directions and headed toward the restroom, I came across a tiny plastic heart with the word "love" inscribed on it. As I picked it up and put it in my pocket, God spoke to my heart: "Don't try to understand so much; just love. Love me, and let my love flow through you to others. It really is that simple, my daughter."

It was the first time He spoke to me about how simple His message really is. I had been confused and contemplating spiritual things all day, and all He wanted me to do was to love Him and love others. God spoke to me through a little plastic heart, but what the heart represented was the greatest gift of all, His love.

I carry that plastic heart with me in my planner everywhere I go. Since that time, I have found many little hearts on the ground. I always pick them up, smile at God, and remember the simple message of love He spoke to me that day.

God as Peace

Another time I was walking on a trail close to my home and found myself at a big open field that looked very familiar. I had never been on this trail before, and as I looked around, I couldn't believe how similar it was to the happy healing place I had created in my mind (this is the place I guide you to on my "A Breath ~ in Stillness" CD, Track 4). I visualize this healing place often to feel the presence of God.

I went into the middle of the field, dropped to my knees and started crying. I was completely overwhelmed by the power of God that day. It was like I had been there before, and now I was actually seeing in person what I had visualized in my head for so long. It was truly unbelievable, something only God could have done.

God has proven Himself faithful over and over in my life. He is the steady, peaceful presence in the midst of life's inevitable distractions. My prayer is that you will allow Him to prove Himself faithful to you. Allow Him access to your heart and mind, and trust Him to heal you.

AFTERWORD

I believe with my heart, mind and spirit that Jesus Christ is the Way, the Truth and the Life. Surrendering to Him and allowing Him into every aspect of my life has been the most amazing journey I have ever experienced.

I am not a Bible thumper or a "religious" person in any way. I simply desire to radiate the love of Christ in my life so that others can experience His unconditional love through me. My journey is very simple—it is all about love. I want to be so filled with God's love that I can't help but to *be love* and *give love* to those around me. It really is that simple.

I do not want to compel you to love Jesus using fear or to push you into a relationship with Him out of guilt or condemnation. I want to reflect Jesus' life by the way I live, and trust that He will draw you to Himself as only He can. Allow yourself to turn toward Him and open your heart to His unconditional love. He will meet you right where you are with His offer of unique healing. Accept it, and watch your life transform. Surrender everything you are to Him, and He will empower you to live the life He has specially designed for you. Join me on this journey to *be love* and *give love* to the world around us.

"Your love for one another will prove to the world that you are my disciples"
John 13:35 (NLT)

Follow Abby Online
Book Speaking Engagements

www.myjourneytohealing.com

ABOUT THE AUTHOR

Abby Lewis has a degree in Health and Wellness and her massage therapy license. Her life's work is to passionately encourage others to climb out of their own dark valleys by finding health of spirit, mind and body. Abby, her husband, and their son live in Branson, Missouri.

APPENDIX A

The Science behind Walking in Peace

About two years ago, a client and dear friend shared some information with me that I was very blessed to receive. The information resonated with my spirit and confirmed all that God had placed on my heart about the power of our thought lives and the importance of living out of peace and love. I began doing research on the information my friend gave me—the book by Dr. Caroline Leaf called *Who Switched off my Brain? Controlling Toxic Thoughts and Emotions. Revised edition.*[1]

I was so excited to find that there is scientific proof to back up what I had suspected all along—that living a life of peace not only feels good, but actually transforms us physiologically. Now, when I share this information, along with my personal testimony, people are often alarmed to realize they are destroying their bodies from the inside out. But, they also now understand the power of choosing to take minutes, hours, and even days to be still with God so that they can develop a life of walking in peace.

Since 1981, Dr. Caroline Leaf, a strong follower of Jesus Christ, has researched the human brain with particular emphasis on unlocking its vast untapped potential. According to Dr. Leaf, research indicates that "up to 80% of physical, emotional and mental health issues today could be a direct result of our thought lives."[2]

Dr. Leaf explains how research done by neuroscientists and biochemists tell us that when we think negative thoughts, our brains release chemicals in the wrong amount upsetting the electrical-chemical balance, which creates inflammation or literal damage in the area in and around the thought. She calls these "toxic trees." By contrast, positive thoughts actually create healthy trees (nerve networks or thought networks) in the brain. She says that we can choose to re-shape our brains by going through a process of thought detoxification:

> Detoxifying your thoughts can be like selecting a book from a shelf in your library of memories, rewriting a page in that book, then placing it back on the shelf, free of toxic thoughts and emotions. If it happens to be a life-threatening book, you may want to do even more work on it and even get rid of the book altogether. That is part of the process of building a new, healthy thought over an old, toxic one and removing the negative emotional sting at the same time. The good news is we can change those pathways and create new ones within twenty-one days![3]

One of the elements she mentions in this healing process is repentance and forgiveness. Dr. Leaf explains that "forgiveness is a choice, an act of your free will. It enables you to release all those toxic thoughts of anger, resentment, bitterness, shame, grief, regret, guilt and hate. These emotions hold your mind in a nasty, vice-like grip. As long as these unhealthy toxic thoughts dominate your mind, you will not be able to grow healthy new thoughts and memories. . . . When people hold onto their anger and past trauma, the stress response stays active, making them sick mentally and physically."[4]

Congruence between what we think and what we speak is imperative if we wish to grow new memory trees to overcome the toxic trees, which are alive and destroying mental and physical health. She says, "Science clearly demonstrates the link between your thoughts and emotions, and your physical and mental well-being. The more you manage your thought life and emotions, the more you will learn to listen to your thoughts and deal constructively with them, and the more balanced and life-giving your emotions will become."[5] For optimal health, we must make a conscious effort to get our toxic emotions under control.

Dr. Leaf tells us in her book that this is especially important in light of new research showing that the heart contains 40,000 neurons that work in a feedback loop to our brains! This "brain in your heart acts like a checking station for all the emotions generated by the flow of chemicals created by thoughts. It is proving to be a real intelligent force behind the intuitive thoughts and feelings you experience."[6]

This physiological truth reflects biblical teaching on the connection between our hearts, thoughts, words and actions. Jesus said, "But the things that come out of the mouth come from the heart, and these make a man unclean. For out of the heart come evil thoughts, murder, adultery, sexual immorality, theft, false testimony, slander" (Matthew 15:18–19). Similarly He says, "For out of the overflow of the heart the mouth speaks" (Matthew 12:34). Paul exhorts us to "be transformed by the renewing of your mind" (Romans 12:2) and to think about "whatever is true, whatever is noble, whatever is right, whatever is pure, whatever is lovely, whatever is admirable- if anything is excellent or praiseworthy" (Philippians 4:8).

To sum up the research, negative thoughts create toxic trees in our brains. When the toxic trees are present, they create a toxic chemical flood that is released into our body creating disease, pain and dysfunction. Living a life representative of the fruit of the spirit (love, joy, peace, patience, kindness, goodness, faithfulness, gentleness and self-control), along with forgiveness, starts repairing and healing the toxic trees in twenty-one days.

When we rewire the toxic trees (renewing of the mind), the toxic chemical flood stops and healing takes place within our spirits, our minds and our bodies. To read the research for yourself, or to learn more, you can visit www.drleaf.net.

APPENDIX B

"A Breath ~ in Stillness" CD

In June of 2009, God led me to create "A Breath ~ in Stillness," a healing CD designed to assist you in establishing a life of stillness.

- Track 1 is a short introduction to the CD.

- Track 2 uses a powerful exercise that will guide you through the process of releasing the burdens you are carrying in order to allow God's love to flow through your life.

- Track 3 shares how God helped me heal through gratitude and gives an example of an exercise you may choose to do as well.

- Track 4 guides you through a relaxation exercise that will help you find peace when you are experiencing any sort of stress or anxiety.

The more you listen to the CD, the more powerful your experience will become. As you learn to utilize it to reach a place of peace and rest with God, you will find healing and freedom. I recommend listening to the CD daily in the beginning. Then, as your life begins to transform and you develop a practice of stillness with God on your own, I recommend listening to "A Breath ~ in Stillness" whenever you need a refresher or need assistance finding stillness with God.

To listen to a sample clip from "A Breath ~ in Stillness," visit the "Healing CD" link on my website, www.myjourneytohealing.com.

APPENDIX C

Food Chart[1]

Food Category	Food	Rating <-- highly acidic -- highly alkaline -->					
Breads	Corn Tortillas		x				
Breads	Rye bread			x			
Breads	Sourdough bread		x				
Breads	White biscuit			x			
Breads	White bread		x				
Breads	Whole-grain bread			x			
Breads	Whole-meal bread			x			
Condiments	Ketchup		x				
Condiments	Mayonnaise		x				
Condiments	Miso		x				
Condiments	Mustard		x				
Condiments	Soy sauce		x				
Dairy	Buttermilk				x		
Dairy	Cheese (all varieties, from all milks)		x				
Dairy	Cream			x			
Dairy	Egg whites		x				

Category	Item	1	2	3	4	5	6
Dairy	Eggs (whole)		x				
Dairy	Homogenized milk			x			
Dairy	Milk (not pasteurized)			x			
Dairy	Milk (pasteurized)		x				
Dairy	Paneer (cheese)		x				
Dairy	Quark		x				
Dairy	Yoghurt (sweetened)		x				
Dairy	Yoghurt (unsweetened)			x			
Beverages & Drinks	Beer	x					
Beverages & Drinks	Coffee	x					
Beverages & Drinks	Coffee substitute drinks			x			
Beverages & Drinks	Fruit juice (natural)			x			
Beverages & Drinks	Fruit juice (sweetened)	x					
Beverages & Drinks	Liquor	x					
Beverages & Drinks	Soda/Pop		x				
Beverages & Drinks	Tea (black)	x					
Beverages & Drinks	Tea (herbal, green)				x		
Beverages & Drinks	Water (Fiji, Hawaiian, Evian)				x		
Beverages & Drinks	Water (sparkling)		x				
Beverages & Drinks	Water (spring)			x			
Beverages & Drinks	Wine		x				
Fats & Oils	Borage oil				x		
Fats & Oils	Butter			x			
Fats & Oils	Coconut Oil (raw)				x		
Fats & Oils	Cod liver oil			x			
Fats & Oils	Corn oil			x			
Fats & Oils	Evening Primrose oil				x		
Fats & Oils	Flax seed oil				x		
Fats & Oils	Margarine			x			
Fats & Oils	Marine lipids				x		
Fats & Oils	Olive Oil				x		
Fats & Oils	Sesame oil				x		
Fats & Oils	Sunflower oil			x			

Fruits	Acai Berry			x		
Fruits	Apples			x		
Fruits	Apricot			x		
Fruits	Apricots			x		
Fruits	Apricots (dried)			x		
Fruits	Avocado (protein)					x
Fruits	Banana (ripe)		x			
Fruits	Banana (unripe)				x	
Fruits	Black currant			x		
Fruits	Blackberries			x		
Fruits	Blueberry			x		
Fruits	Cantaloupe			x		
Fruits	Cherry, sour				x	
Fruits	Cherry, sweet			x		
Fruits	Clementine's			x		
Fruits	Coconut, fresh				x	
Fruits	Cranberry			x		
Fruits	Currant			x		
Fruits	Dates			x		
Fruits	Dates (dried)			x		
Fruits	Fig juice powder			x		
Fruits	Figs (dried)				x	
Fruits	Figs (raw)				x	
Fruits	Fresh lemon				x	
Fruits	Goji berries			x		
Fruits	Gooseberry, ripe			x		
Fruits	Grapefruit			x		
Fruits	Grapes (ripe)			x		
Fruits	Italian plum			x		
Fruits	Limes				x	
Fruits	Mandarin orange		x			
Fruits	Mango			x		
Fruits	Nectarine			x		

Category	Food						
Fruits	Orange			x			
Fruits	Papaya			x			
Fruits	Peach			x			
Fruits	Pear			x			
Fruits	Pineapple		x				
Fruits	Pomegranate		x				
Fruits	Raspberry		x				
Fruits	Red currant			x			
Fruits	Rose hips		x				
Fruits	Strawberries			x			
Fruits	Strawberry			x			
Fruits	Tangerine			x			
Fruits	Tomato					x	
Fruits	Watermelon			x			
Fruits	Yellow plum			x			
Grains & Legumes	Basmati rice			x			
Grains & Legumes	Brown rice		x				
Grains & Legumes	Buckwheat				x		
Grains & Legumes	Bulgur wheat			x			
Grains & Legumes	Couscous			x			
Grains & Legumes	Granulated soy (cooked, ground)					x	
Grains & Legumes	Kamut				x		
Grains & Legumes	Lentils				x		
Grains & Legumes	Lima beans					x	
Grains & Legumes	Oats			x			
Grains & Legumes	Rye bread			x			
Grains & Legumes	Soy flour				x		
Grains & Legumes	Soy lecithin, pure						x
Grains & Legumes	Soy nuts (soaked soy beans, then dried)						x
Grains & Legumes	Soybeans, fresh					x	
Grains & Legumes	Spelt				x		

Category	Food					
Grains & Legumes	Tofu				x	
Grains & Legumes	Wheat		x			
Grains & Legumes	White (navy) beans					x
Meat, Poultry & Fish	Beef	x				
Meat, Poultry & Fish	Buffalo		x			
Meat, Poultry & Fish	Chicken		x			
Meat, Poultry & Fish	Duck		x			
Meat, Poultry & Fish	Fresh water fish		x			
Meat, Poultry & Fish	Liver			x		
Meat, Poultry & Fish	Ocean fish		x			
Meat, Poultry & Fish	Organ meats			x		
Meat, Poultry & Fish	Oysters			x		
Meat, Poultry & Fish	Pork	x				
Meat, Poultry & Fish	Sardines (canned)	x				
Meat, Poultry & Fish	Tuna (canned)	x				
Meat, Poultry & Fish	Veal	x				
Meat, Poultry & Fish	Wild salmon,		x			
Misc	Apple Cider Vinegar			x		
Misc	Baking soda					x
Misc	Bee pollen				x	
Misc	Canned foods		x			
Misc	Cereals (like Kellogg's etc)		x			

Category	Food						
Misc	Hummus			x			
Misc	Microwave foods		x				
Misc	Popcorn			x			
Misc	Rice milk			x			
Misc	Royal Jelly				x		
Misc	Soy Protein Powder			x			
Misc	Tempeh			x			
Misc	Whey protein powder			x			
Nuts	Almond				x		
Nuts	Almond butter (raw)				x		
Nuts	Brazil nuts			x			
Nuts	Cashews			x			
Nuts	Filberts			x			
Nuts	Hazelnut			x			
Nuts	Macadamia nuts (raw)			x			
Nuts	Peanut butter (raw, organic)		x				
Nuts	Peanuts		x				
Nuts	Pine nuts (raw)				x		
Nuts	Pistachios		x				
Nuts	Walnuts			x			
Roots	Carrot				x		
Roots	Fresh red beet					x	
Roots	Kohlrabi				x		
Roots	Potatoes				x		
Roots	Red radish					x	
Roots	Rutabaga				x		
Roots	Summer black radish						x
Roots	Sweet potatoes			x			
Roots	Turnip				x		
Roots	White radish (spring)				x		
Roots	Yams				x		
Seeds	Barley			x			
Seeds	Caraway seeds				x		

Category	Item						
Seeds	Cumin seeds				x		
Seeds	Fennel seeds				x		
Seeds	Flax seeds			x			
Seeds	Pumpkin seeds			x			
Seeds	Sesame seeds				x		
Seeds	Sunflower seeds			x			
Seeds	Wheat Kernel		x				
Sweets & Sweeteners	Agave nectar			x			
Sweets & Sweeteners	Alcohol sugars (xylitol and the other sacharides)		x				
Sweets & Sweeteners	Artificial sweeteners	x					
Sweets & Sweeteners	Barley malt syrup			x			
Sweets & Sweeteners	Beet sugar		x				
Sweets & Sweeteners	Brown rice syrup			x			
Sweets & Sweeteners	Chocolates		x				
Sweets & Sweeteners	Dr. Bronner's barley malt sweetener			x			
Sweets & Sweeteners	Dried sugar cane juice			x			
Sweets & Sweeteners	Fructose			x			
Sweets & Sweeteners	Halva [ground sesame seed sweet]		x				
Sweets & Sweeteners	Honey			x			
Sweets & Sweeteners	Maple Syrup			x			
Sweets & Sweeteners	Milk sugar			x			
Sweets & Sweeteners	Molasses		x				

Category	Item						
Sweets & Sweeteners	Sugar (white)		x				
Sweets & Sweeteners	Sugarcane		x				
Sweets & Sweeteners	Turbinado sugar			x			
Sweets & Sweeteners	Xylitol		x				
Vegetables	Alfalfa					x	
Vegetables	Alfalfa grass						x
Vegetables	Artichokes				x		
Vegetables	Asparagus				x		
Vegetables	Aubergine/Egg plant				x		
Vegetables	Barley grass						x
Vegetables	Basil				x		
Vegetables	Bell peppers/capsicums (all colors)				x		
Vegetables	Blue-Green Algae			x			
Vegetables	Bok Choy				x		
Vegetables	Brussels sprouts				x		
Vegetables	Cabbage lettuce, fresh					x	
Vegetables	Canned vegetables		x				
Vegetables	Cauliflower				x		
Vegetables	Cayenne pepper					x	
Vegetables	Celery					x	
Vegetables	Chives				x		
Vegetables	Cilantro					x	
Vegetables	Comfrey				x		
Vegetables	Cooked vegetables (all kinds)			x			
Vegetables	Cucumber, fresh						x
Vegetables	Dandelion						x
Vegetables	Dog grass						x
Vegetables	Endive, fresh					x	
Vegetables	French cut (green) beans					x	

Category	Item						
Vegetables	Frozen vegetables		x				
Vegetables	Garlic					x	
Vegetables	Ginger					x	
Vegetables	Ginseng				x		
Vegetables	Green cabbage, (December Harvest)				x		
Vegetables	Green cabbage, (March Harvest)				x		
Vegetables	Horse radish				x		
Vegetables	Jicama						x
Vegetables	Kale						x
Vegetables	Kamut grass						x
Vegetables	Lamb's lettuce				x		
Vegetables	Leeks (bulbs)				x		
Vegetables	Lettuce				x		
Vegetables	Mushrooms		x				
Vegetables	Mustard greens				x		
Vegetables	Onion				x		
Vegetables	Oregano					x	
Vegetables	Parsnips				x		
Vegetables	Peas, fresh				x		
Vegetables	Peas, ripe				x		
Vegetables	Peppers				x		
Vegetables	Pickled vegetables	x					
Vegetables	Pumpkins (raw)				x		
Vegetables	Raw onions				x		
Vegetables	Red cabbage				x		
Vegetables	Rhubarb stalks				x		
Vegetables	Savoy Cabbage				x		
Vegetables	Sea Vegetables				x		
Vegetables	Seaweed (dulse, kelp, laver, etc)				x		
Vegetables	Shave grass						x
Vegetables	Sorrel					x	

Vegetables	Sourkraut		x				
Vegetables	Soy Sprouts						x
Vegetables	Spinach (March harvest)				x		
Vegetables	Spinach (other than March)					x	
Vegetables	Sprouted seeds (all kinds)						x
Vegetables	Squash (all kinds, raw)				x		
Vegetables	Straw grass						x
Vegetables	Thyme				x		
Vegetables	Tomatoes (puree)				x		
Vegetables	Tomatoes (raw)				x		
Vegetables	Tomatoes (sundried)				x		
Vegetables	Watercress				x		
Vegetables	Wheat grass						x
Vegetables	White cabbage				x		
Vegetables	Yeast			x			
Vegetables	Zucchini				x		

END NOTES

Chapter 1

1. Reprinted by permission. Lucado, Max. *The Applause of Heaven* (Nashville, Tennessee: Thomas Nelson Inc., 1999, All rights reserved), p. 23–24.

Chapter 11

1. Information in this section adapted with permission from http://acidalkalinediet.com [accessed 5-22-10].

2. Information in this section is a paraphrase of an online article by Tsang, R.D., Gloria. "Antioxidants 101," http://www.healthcastle.com/antioxidant.shtml [accessed 9-20-10].

3. Oz, Dr. Mehmet, "Food Hall of Fame . . . and Shame," http://www.oprah.com/health/Dr-Ozs-Food-Hall-of-Shame-and-Fame [accessed 4-24-10].

Appendix A

1. Leaf, Dr. Caroline. *Who Switched off my Brain? Controlling Toxic Thoughts and Emotions. Revised Edition* (Thomas Nelson Publishers, 2009)

2. Ibid., p. 15

3. Ibid., p. 46

4. Ibid., p. 109

5. Ibid., p. 43

6. Ibid., p. 40

Appendix C

1. The Alkaline Diet, http://acidalkalinediet.com [accessed 5-22-10]